YOU ARE A DOG

# YOU ARE A DOG

*Life Through the Eyes of*

*Man's Best Friend*

TERRY BAIN

*Harmony Books*

NEW YORK

For more of life through the eyes of man's best friend, please
visit the *You Are a Dog* website at www.youareadog.com
(where you can e-mail the author and his dogs).

Copyright © 2004 by Terry Bain

All images used by permission.
Copyright Arts Parts (http://ronandjoe.com/).

Published by Harmony Books, New York, New York. Member of
the Crown Publishing Group, a division of Random House, Inc.
www.crownpublishing.com

HARMONY BOOKS is a registered trademark and the
Harmony Books colophon is a trademark of Random House, Inc.

Portions of *You Are a Dog* have previously appeared on
sweetfancymoses.com.

Printed in the United States of America

*Design by Lynne Amft*

Library of Congress Cataloging-in-Publication Data
Bain, Terry.
You are a dog : life through the eyes of man's
best friend / Terry Bain.—1st ed.
1. Dogs.   I. Title.
SF426.2.B34   2004
636.7—dc22   2004018137

ISBN 1-4000-5242-4

10 9 8 7 6 5 4 3 2

First Edition

*Grace*

*June 1, 2003*

# ACKNOWLEDGMENTS

When writing acknowledgments for this book, I am most confounded by order. Whom do I thank first, my wife or my dog? My dog or my wife? Do I put them at the beginning or at the end? But it is questions like these that Sarah—my wife—will find easy to answer (Why are you spending so much time agonizing over the acknowledgments? . . . Just write them, for crying out loud.), so Sarah, thank you first and foremost, because without you I would likely still be writing Chapter Four.

Then my children, of course, in order of appearance: Carver, Sophia, and Grace. I cannot remember what sort of writer I was before all of you arrived, but I seem to remember a far more self-absorbed writer—someone who would dismiss the impulse to write a book about dogs because he's working on his "art." Well, here's your art, and it's a dog book, and thank God.

Thank you to the people of St. Mark's Lutheran Church for providing me with space to write and for other unquantifiable blessings.

Matt Herlihy, you had the wisdom (or stupidity) to publish the seed of this book in your very funny online magazine, Sweet Fancy Moses (http://sweetfancymoses. com). I did not, at the time, think I was writing a book. Did I get carried away or what?

ACKNOWLEDGMENTS

Shaye, you said yes, you would publish my book. How can I truly thank you enough? More treats for Ella? They'll be on their way soon enough. Kim, you manage to put up with persnickety writers like myself for a living. Clearly you will be sainted (or, at the very least, subtitled). You always sound happy to hear from me, no matter how ridiculous my complaint or how minuscule my query. And Julie, I have a feeling that without your able assistance, all the rest would come crashing down.

Super-agent Jenny Bent, your enthusiasm for *You Are a Dog* has always been second to none. You gave me the confidence to think of *You Are a Dog* as a real book, not just an idea in my head that was kind of funny and a bit of a lark. May all kinds of good fortune come your way.

And finally, Pretzel. I will put you at the end because you are a dog. And I'm only going to say this one more time. . . . I cannot throw the ball for you unless you drop it. So drop it. And stop looking at me like that with those big dog eyes.

Thank you. All of you. May you all be blessed with good friends who have the sense to know when it's time to go home and good dogs who have the sense to know when it's time to come closer.

# CONTENTS

# CONTENTS

# I

## IDENTIFYING YOU

Y ou are somewhat embarrassed. An entire book? About you? What must have they been thinking?

### N A M E

They call you Dog. They call you Rex and Rover and Spike and Ishmael. You are Clive and Spot and Sparky and Belvedere and Lucy and Gracie and Princess. And you are none of these. You are just you. You have only one name for yourself. It has no translation into speakable, human words, but if it were translated into speakable, human words, it would come closest to "You."

You do not identify yourself with the other names that have been given you (Jack, Bootsie, Stanley, Sadie, Blackie, Patrice), by your people or by others (Ruff Ruff, Pretzel, Duchess), though you do recognize that these are meant to be names, of a sort, but in that troubling language that makes little sense to you. You wonder, sometimes, how people communicate at all.

These are some of the names that have recently been given you that, though not your true name, are human approximations, and you admit that though humans are confusing and confounding, they are worth having, so you respond to these names immediately and enthusiastically. Here they are. Not all of them. Just some of them. Here:

### Dog

Not actually a name so much as a designation, your people, or some other people who are not your people, will nevertheless call you this upon occasion, and it is one of the names you recognize. She Who Seldom Drops Food on the Floor might say something like this: "You are a dog." You are sitting before her, waiting for her to drop food on the floor. You are in the kitchen, examining the process of slicing cheese. She Who Seldom Drops Food on the Floor is slicing cheese and placing the slices into sandwiches for the children (and sandwiches for the children are always a good source of found or otherwise coerced food).

She does not throw you a slice of cheese. Instead she crosses the kitchen and says, "You are a dog." She comes directly toward you, and you watch her closely. "Move," she says. She pushes you out of the way because she knows that if she doesn't, you will continue to wait there and she won't be able to get to the sink. When she returns to the cutting board from the sink, you are sitting instead in front of the cutting board. "Ack," she says. "I said," she says, "didn't you hear me . . . ? Go lie down. I'm not giving you any cheese." She pushes you again—a nudge, actually, with her knee—and tosses a corner of cheese into the dining room that she knows you will follow. Apparently you did just what she wanted you to do. Cheese is your favorite and most treasured reward.

## Pup

They sometimes call you Pup. You pretend not to know that the name is diminutive, that it means anything other than respect and love. Which is, of course, exactly what it means. You can tell by the intonation that the name is diminutive, that it is affectionate. Especially when He Who Calls You Pup calls you Pup, when he rubs your head and calls you Pup and then scratches your jowls and puts his face in your face, at which time you lick his cheeks and nose (and he often allows this), still scratching, still making the sound that comes from somewhere deep inside him that means, "love love and love." He can call you whatever he likes and you will lick him and he will feed you and call you Pup.

## Pooch

Of all the names. What does this mean? You don't like the sound of it, though you try not to show that you don't like the sound of it. Seldom will you show any kind of offense to this name. Seldom, actually, do you show any kind of offense to anything, except when offense is first offered by a cat. Then you will return the utmost offense to the cat by ignoring her. The cat does not understand this as offense, though, because cats, though beautiful, are crazy.

## Mutt

What? Do they know who they are talking to? Mutt? Did he say Mutt? Or did he drop something? What was that? What an odd thing. Is that a name? It sounds like a noise. Like an expression of what it is. Like a dropped wet towel. What an odd thing.

## Sound

They have another name for you that they use most often (Sam, Chevy, Pete), and you understand this is what they think your real name is (Sheba, Abby, Nestle). You know that when they call you this name and you come to them immediately, you will receive some kind of reward from one of your people, such as their attention or a handful of kibble or a small cut-up piece of hot dog (though this last is very rare).

Except, of course, sometimes you will not get a reward. Sometimes when they call you and you think you are going to be rewarded, they are actually going to put you outside because they are leaving for the day and they expect you to stay outside without them. They will be gone all day, and they tell you this in their ridiculous people language, so that you do not know what it is they are saying . . . though you understand the tone of voice means they are leaving, and you imagine they will be gone for many many years, and in fact you may never see them again, so you go to the gate and you lie where you can be seen as they leave but where it will not be suspected that you plan to escape or chew a child's toy into such small pieces that the toy will be unidentifiable. You are deciding now, as they leave, if you should choose escape or toy. Escape or toy.

Has it been a few moments since they've been gone or a few hours?

What's the difference? And what is that?

Water falling from the sky.

You are being punished for your thoughts. You must ask for forgiveness. You must seek shelter.

## THE HOURS

You have been outside for many hours. It has rained, but now the sun is out and the wind is blow-
ing. You bite at the wind. You wait at the gate when you are not barking at a cat or squirrel or tree branch. They will be home any minute or they will be gone for days. They will be gone forever, and you will never be fed again and you will have to find your own food. Every minute you are aware that they might never return. Every minute you are aware that they could be home any second. Any second now. Is that them? No. Not them. Still not them.

## MEMORY

You are the original dog. You are every dog and no dog. What kind of dog are you? You are the kind who can remember your ancestors, can remember your mother, can remember your mother's mother, can remember your mother's mother's mother. It is not difficult to have this kind of memory. You understand that it is difficult for many species to remember. But for you it is impossible to think of yourself without thinking of all your past, of the village mothers and fathers who were original dogs, original people companions, living with and alongside and among the people. Helping them. You know that you are helping. You are glad to be helping. What would they be without you?

Some dogs, you know, find it difficult to remember their past, to have any kind of relationship with Those Who Came Before. Some of these dogs are even distantly related to you, but they do not recognize this, and therefore do not indicate any knowledge of common ancestry. You wish you could show them somehow that there is no need to forget everything just to live with humans. There is no need to act so stupid.

You wonder if they can live full lives without this memory. You wonder if something is missing in them. Something quintessentially *dog* must be missing. You always treat these dogs as nicely as possible, and you try not to stare. You feel sorry for them, and you hope it doesn't show when you do stare, or you hope it doesn't show that you are trying not to stare when you are trying not to stare.

## YOUR PEOPLE

To keep track of your people, you have many names for them. Most of these names are sense names. They are sight and sound and smell names. Again, these cannot be truly translated, but you have some reasonable approximations, which you are happy to share.

*Your People's Names*

*Your People*

*Those Who Would Bathe You*

*He Who Would Bathe You Quickly So as to Get It Over With*

*Those Who Would Feed You*

*Those Who Would Pet You*

*He Who Would Scratch Unscratchable Places*

*She Who Would Walk You Off the Lead*

*He Who Would Throw the Ball but for Whom You Will Not Drop the Ball*

*She Who Would Refill the Water Dish*

*He Who Smells of Garlic, Tastes of Salt, and Will Let You Lick His Feet*

*She Who Does Not Allow Licking Ever*

*She Who Drops Food from Her Plate*

*He Who Leaves the Seat Up So That You Might Drink*

## S E N S E N A M E S

Dog names are too complex as translated into the language of your people. Though each is translated into words above, to prevent confusion, there are no real "words" associated with each name in your mind, and the concept of a name being translated into words is foreign to you. The association is sense only, and the sense is remembered in the organ that senses it: odor in your nose or touch on your skin or taste on your tongue or sight in your eyes or sound in your ears or knowledge (gnosis) way deep down in your dogness.

## T H E   S E N S E   O F   G N O S I S

You have a sense that you are pretty sure your people do not have, and it is the sense of gnosis, or knowledge. It is difficult to describe to those who do not experience it firsthand, but it is the most reliable of all your senses. You feel it in the most reliable of places. You feel it in the part of you that makes you You. You feel it in your dogness. You are a dog, and all dogs have this sense, and all dogs have access to this dogness. Not all dogs use this access, however; it has been worn away by time and the lack of need for it. It has been worn away by indiscriminate and unlikely misuse.

## Y O U R  P E O P L E

Each of your people has several individual sense names, but this is not
confusing to you, because it is not a
matter for your brain, as you've already
mentioned, but a matter of sense
memory.

### *He Who Leaves the Seat Up So That You Might Drink*

This is your favorite name for him, though he, too, has
many. When you are downstairs, alone, and headed toward
the bathroom, you hope that he has been the last to use
the seat. Often, he has. Each night, this is generally the last
name you give him before going to bed, and this name will
be on your mind when you wake. At this time he becomes
He Who Lets You Outside So That You May Pee.
Sometimes you have to wake him so that he will let you
out so that you can pee. If this is the case, before he is He
Who Lets You Outside So That You May Pee, he is first
He Who Pushes You Away Saying, "Dammit, Don't Lick
My Damn Face."

### *She Who Pretends to Be Angry When You Jump Onto the Bed to Greet Her*

When you jump onto the bed to greet her, she uses the
voice that is supposed to mean she is angry, or the voice
that is supposed to tell you that though she's using the

voice that is supposed to tell you that she's angry, the voice instead means that she does not mind that you've just jumped up onto the bed, and it will be up to someone else to call you down. You sometimes think of her as She Who Means Little but Implies Much.

When you jump onto the bed, the children follow you up, and the cat disappears, and you are all up there in the warmth and the glory, and you will stay there until it becomes clear that the children's antics are going to cause an injury soon, at which point you jump down and go to the closed bathroom door, hoping that whoever used the bathroom last left the seat up, hoping that someone will leave the door open soon. You are so thirsty.

### The Baby

The Baby is also known as She Who Would Climb Over You While You Sleep. She is also She Who Would Pull Your Ears for No Reason Other Than the Pleasure of Pulling Your Ears, and She Who Randomly Flings Food from the Table. She Who Would Climb Over You While You Sleep is a name you use for her as you select a place to lie down. In reality, this name is no longer or shorter than any of the other names, since it is not made up of words but of your emotional response to sensory data. As you are looking for a place to lie down, you are sometimes thinking, *Find a place where She Who Would Climb Over You While You Sleep will not climb over you or pull on your ears or otherwise stumble into you.* The thinking of these thoughts and the feeling of the emotions associated with them are inseparable, and the name The Baby does not conflict with She Who Would Climb Over You While You Sleep. They are, in effect, the same name.

It should also be noted that there is no such place in the house where she will not climb over you or pull on your ears or otherwise bump into you and wake you up, but you look for it, you search for it, you long for it. Until she actually does climb over you or pull on your ears or otherwise bump into you. Then you are filled with joy at her presence and you lick her face. She has the most flavorful, ever-changing face of all your people. Sometimes salt (good). Sometimes apple (okay). Sometimes peas (yuck). Sometimes milk (yum).

It should also be noted that though The Baby belongs to you, she is not yours. Though she belongs to you, you are not confused. She is not a puppy.

### He Who Rides His Bicycle in the Driveway

He also has many other names, such as He Who Puts You Outside When His Friends Visit, or He Who Puts You Inside When He and His Friends Play Outside or He Who Leaps from the Furniture. Most of the time, he pretends to ignore you. But you know better. He picked you from the box and held you first. His scent is imprinted on you, and above all, you will protect him from all harm. Your relationship with him is somewhere between brother and pack leader and father.

21

Although he, too, belongs to you, and of all your people is most like you, he is not of you.

## OTHERS OUTSIDE THE HOUSEHOLD

There are many others. Some of the others you know well and some of the others you do not know well. When you do not know them, they are simply The Others. If you do know them, you have a sense name for them.

## OTHERS WITH NAMES

Most of the others to whom you refer with sense names have only one. Some have greater roles in your life than others, but they still generally only have one sense name. The following is a short list of examples.

### *He Who Lives Next Door and Who Bites Your Ears*

Sometimes you are left with He Who Lives Next Door and Who Bites Your Ears when your people are away. You encourage this, as he is your favorite of all the people who are not your people. However, while you are in his care you are also frantic that your people may never return. You adore He Who Lives Next Door and Who Bites Your Ears, but he could never replace your people. He Who Lives Next Door and Who Bites Your Ears is not, after all, He Who Chose You from the Box of Your Siblings, so there is no comparing him to your people. It is too bad, too, because he really seems to understand how to communicate with you like no other. You have never struggled to be understood by him. He just seems to know.

## The Deliverer of Unknowable Packages

Sometimes this person—who drives a large, rectangular brown truck—changes forms, and is apparently different people, but you know better. He (or she, you are not quite sure) always wears the same brown uniform, carries a package of some sort to the front door of the house, and will leave this package behind even (or especially) if your people are not home. He (or she) always smells of mystery, of exotic everywhere and you can smell him (or her) even from a distance. You bark and you bark and you bark and you bark. Sometimes this elicits a minor response, sometimes not. Seldom, however, does the Deliverer of Unknowable Packages flee.

## She Who Smells of Innumerable Cats

She lives somewhere nearby. Next door? Across the street? You see her everywhere, it seems, and you sometimes meet the cats of whom she smells, though they only appear at a distance. How is this possible that she smells of all those cats? Do they all live with her? Is she really a cat in disguise?

### Woman Who Sometimes Brings Small Fluffy Friend

When Woman Who Brings Small Fluffy Friend brings Small Fluffy Friend (who is of your species but somehow so much smaller than you and looks nothing at all like you except for his eyes, if you examine them close to your own eyes, which nobody ever does), you hardly notice that Woman Who Brings Small Fluffy Friend is in the house. If she does not bring Small Fluffy Friend, you jump up and try to push her back through the door to fetch Small Fluffy Friend.

"Off!" she says, pushing you down or crossing her hands in front of her chest or simply turning away from you, turning directly around as if to go and fetch Small Fluffy Friend, but she just stands there. She doesn't go get him.

This isn't working. She's not going back to retrieve Small Fluffy Friend. Apparently, she's forgotten where she left Small Fluffy Friend. You go to the dark wood hutch that you sometimes lie against and watch her in case she heads for the door. You sense that she's hiding something. All the while she's here, your eyes will not leave her, and though you see every move she makes, you learn nothing.

### Man Who Stings Your Hip

Though it is a short drive, you regret their having taken you to Man Who Stings Your Hip. The shortness of the drive is no consolation for the sting, which is not so much about pain as it is about surprise. You do not like surprise. Neither is the dog biscuit much of a consolation.

Luckily, you have not seen Man Who Stings Your Hip in a very long time. There is time enough between visits now that you are not always thinking of him and the sting that he gives you. Maybe now your people have forgotten about him as well. Just maybe.

## Woman Who Has Replaced Man Who Stings Your Hip

Recently you have visited Woman Who Has Replaced Man Who Stings Your Hip. She has a nice voice, and the drive is longer, which gives you plenty of time to wonder where it is you're going, to memorize the trip for next time. While you are there, and before she stings your hip, she also fills your ear with liquid and rubs your ear and— oh, doesn't that feel good?

Once she came to the house to sting your hip and look into your ears (though she didn't fill them with liquid and she didn't rub them). Has the world gone mad? Why would she come here? Did your people invite her into the house? Did they not know she would do that? What makes them allow this behavior? Your people seem to do unpredictable things at times, things that do not make any kind of sense.

Woman Who Has Replaced Man Who Stings Your Hip seems very friendly with your people, as if she might be a friend or relative, but this cannot be so, can it? You won't believe it. Why would your people consort with such a person?

Perhaps there is a small consolation in this woman. She rubbed your ear after she filled it with liquid, after all, and she taught your people to do the same (though you resist them out of habit whenever they try). And now your ear doesn't itch. And this is a small consolation.

A very small consolation.

## Woman Who Runs with Dog as You Bark

You've never seen her when she wasn't running (though sometimes as she runs past she looks in your direction and smiles, which is an expression you recognize), but you see her almost every day. Sometimes Dog Who Runs with Woman Who Runs with Dog as You Bark returns to your neighborhood by himself, especially after a thunderstorm, and you can smell his passing, his fear. You understand his escape and evacuation, but there's very little you can do. Especially from underneath the bunk beds upstairs.

## Boy Who Once Fed You French Fries but Has Not Fed You Since

This neighborhood boy also passes nearly every day, and sometimes you know he has food. You watch his face to see if he is eating something, and often he is, even when it appears that he is carrying nothing to eat. Sometimes you smell french fries. But he doesn't stop. Just that once he stopped and talked to you and fed you french fries.

Just in case he will stop, you always go to the gate. You always show him how well behaved you are. You always sit for him. For him, you do not bark. He doesn't even say hello. He passes by as if he's never met you before. As if, in some alternate universe, you bit him.

And you have to admit, you have thought of biting him. Why feed you that once? Why only that one time and never again?

But you will not bite him. You will only dream it.

## OTHERS OF YOUR TYPE WHO ARE NOT IN YOUR FAMILY

Others of your type, such as Small Fluffy Friend, you call friends. They will remain friends until they prove themselves otherwise. Until you give them a sense name, they are only called friends. You know they are not of your family, and you know that they are not you, and they look very different, one from the other (mostly, except those that look alike, which you think is very sad, but what can you do?), but they are friends. Though they are friends, if they pass by while the gate is closed, you will bark. You will bark until it is clear they are not coming back. You wish, sometimes, that they would come back. You could use some company. You are not necessarily trying to scare them away, though some of them are scared away. In general they do not come back, especially if they are walking on a lead, pulling a stranger behind them.

## ENEMIES

Real enemies are hard to come by, but you know of at least one.

## Enemy Who Bit You

The dog on the corner near the park attacked you once, breaking free from his lead and, though your only error was (and you recognize this now) looking in his direction and catching his eye, he attacked your hindquarters and your back, once, twice, three times, and you could feel his teeth under your skin, tearing at you until his human reached you and pounced on your attacker. You imagine that having a human pounce on you with all the force of his body would also hurt, and it is a good thing that it did because the teeth were immediately removed from your body and your snarling enemy was dragged away force- fully, trying to bite his own human.

When this happened, She Who Is Stronger Than You Thought, She Who Picked You Up in Her Arms and Carried You Halfway Home took you inside and exam- ined you and she appeared to be crying. Later they loaded you into the car and He Who Takes You to Man Who Stings Your Hip drove the car to Man Who Stings Your Hip, where he stung your hip, where he talked in a sooth- ing voice but you knew all along that he was going to sting your hip. Then he gave you a large biscuit that you had some difficulty eating. Though you weren't cold, you were shivering like a dogsicle. You began to shed your hair and it landed in a halo around you on the cement floor. Your vision seemed to narrow. You imagined yourself falling over, falling down, unable to keep your feet, but you did keep your feet.

You never want to see this Enemy again. You have a sense name now for the enemy that bit you. His sense name is Enemy Who Bit You, and if he is outside his house, you can smell him from over a block away. You smell him and you try to pull the lead across the street. You forget about whoever is on the other end of the lead and you attempt to carry them in the opposite direction.

When you pull the lead away from Enemy's house, hoping that He Who Resists will stop resisting and allow you to cross the street, you sense that He Who Resists is trying to show you something, is trying to teach you something. You do not care. This is a lesson you would just as soon miss.

So far as you can remember, Enemy Who Bit You is your only enemy.

## O T H E R S   W H O   A R E   A N I M A L S

The world is full of activity, of running and jumping and flying things. You do not give animals of other species names (except maybe cats, who are a special kind of animal that you simply do not understand, but who seem to deserve names in certain situations, because they appear to be sentient, however impetuous or odd or just plain crazy).

# 2

# GROWTH AND DISCOVERY

When you compare how quickly you grow with how quickly your people grow, you recognize that there is a difference in your maturity rates. You imagine that this is so you can mature quickly enough to care for the children throughout their lives. And this is what you will do.

## PUPPY

You want to play you want to play you want to play you want to play you want to sleep. You eat. You want to play you want to play you want to play you want to play you want to sleep. You eat. He takes you outside. You respond to this. You smell what it is you have to smell. You don't know yet what it is you have to smell, but you know that you have to smell it. You have to relieve yourself so you do that. What a nice big green place to explore. What a nice big green place to smell.

The back steps are giant. He urges you up the back steps. The back steps are giant and nearly impossible. But you want to play so you try and you try and you try and eventually he picks you up and takes you inside and you want to play you want to play you want to play you want to play you want to sleep.

You sleep. You dream of your mother.

## O B E D I E N C E   C L A S S E S

What are the purposes of these visits? You have a feeling they want you to get something out of them. They feed you in small doses and the other people feed other dogs in small doses. None of the dogs seem to know what it is you are supposed to discover here.

There are a few older dogs, and they simply act when commanded to act, even though the commands don't seem to make any sense. They claim that all it takes is time. They claim that you will never know what the command actually means, but that eventually you will be able to turn the command around, to be fed whenever you want, and not just small doses, but entire meals.

You are skeptical, but you do not complain. These small doses are really quite good. Some of the best food you've ever had, small or not.

### Clicker

Why on earth do they keep making that noise? Maybe if you just do something, anything, and repeat that thing that you did, you can get them to stop. Maybe, but you doubt it. This seems to be reasonably ridiculous behavior by your people, but it doesn't really bother you, especially so long as they keep feeding you these delicious morsels.

## JUDGMENT

You do not judge, though some of the animals of your species think you are the sort who might judge. Enemy Who Bit You, for instance, thinks you judge him. His memory is poor. He does not remember his mother or his mother's mother. You do not judge him—especially not for this. It isn't his fault. You would never judge anyone for anything unless they proved to you that they were unworthy of your friendship, as this dog has. You do not judge him for not knowing his mother or his mother's mother. You do not judge him because he bit you. You simply avoid him, hoping that you never encounter him again.

## DOG DOOR

You do not have one, but you know of dogs that have their own swinging door set into the larger door. You have discussed the possibility of the dog door actually being for the children to use, but they insist that the children use the dog door only when their parents aren't looking. Otherwise they use the larger door.

You refuse to use the dog door. You do not have one in your home, so it must be a kind of insult to the dogs who have them. Are their people so lazy that they cannot let them out the door and in again? Yes. An insult indeed. You do not share these thoughts with your friends. You let them believe whatever they want.

## BOOKS

You have discovered that there are essentially two purposes for books and magazines.

1. They are often used to cover your people's faces, to deny you access to their expressions, so that you will be forced to lie beside them and wait for glimpses of their faces. Often there are pictures on the outside of these books. This is sometimes confusing, especially when the picture is of a dog head. You think there must be some message in this, but you are confounded by what it must mean.

2. They are placed on the sofa while your people are away to keep you from sleeping on the sofa.

## SMILE

When you attempt to reflect the facial expression of your people, you have learned that you are often rewarded with attention, petting, admiration, and sometimes treats. You do this especially when your people have just arrived home and caught you asleep on the sofa. As you get older it is more difficult to get down from the sofa in time to avoid being caught. But if you make a humanlike facial expression, there will be no harsh words for having been caught on the sofa. Instead they might get down on their knees and put their arms around your neck and let you lick their face. Having their arms around your neck is worth it for the opportunity to lick their face.

## LAUGHTER

You have spent a lot of time thinking about it, examining it, listening to it, and thinking some more about it, and you've come to the conclusion that human laughter is okay. It actually seems to improve matters when matters need to be improved. At first you were sure that something was wrong with He Who Laughs at the Television, that you were in some kind of trouble or that he was choking. You thought maybe you would have to save him somehow, and you came near, at first, to see if there was something you could do. Sometimes your nearness just seems to increase the laughter, and this didn't seem good. This didn't seem as if you were solving anything. You were concerned.

But eventually you concluded that human laughter was a spontaneous release of gasses from the human body. They must accumulate a lot of gasses, and this gas must be released.

## AFTER DARK

It's dark. Your people are inside the house. Have they forgotten about you? Do they know you're out here? Don't they know how long the night can be, how many years can pass in a single night?

He's at the back door calling you. He knows. He's looking for you. But how do you tell him you're at the front door? Your method for escape from the backyard—

over the fence at the corner low point, climbing the cyclone fence like a ladder—this does not work in reverse. You've tried it. More than once. When it was clear you needed to be in the backyard. When you were in the front and a cat was in back. When you were in front and your people were in back. When you were in front and nobody was coming for you. Nobody.

Will you be outside all night? Will you lie on the porch and wait for daylight? Will no one find you?

How soon they give up. Has he given up already? So quickly. Don't they love you?

He's gone inside. You paw the screen, hoping he will hear you. Again and again you paw the screen and make the small whining noise that comes from inside somewhere without your calling for it. It is just a noise that comes from you at times like this, and it annoys even you. Again and again. You paw the screen.

### Hours and Hours

How many hours have passed? How many days? How long can you endure this?

A cat!

### Post Chase

You chased the cat but were unsuccessful. You barked and barked and made such a racket that you would think the cat would understand. You have seen this cat before, though you do not know where she lives. You have returned to the porch now and you lie under the porch swing waiting. For some reason it is warmer under the porch swing. This makes a kind of cosmic sense, considering the conservation of energy, as if the energy used in the swing, energy produced by She Who Leaves the House Last swinging slowly and drinking mint tea in the early morning with you at her feet—this energy is stored and contained in the swing, and when it sits motionless, it releases that energy in the form of heat. You receive this heat now and are glad for it, but it is not really enough heat. There is a chill, and even chasing the cat has not warmed you up. That cat. She apparently does not understand. Or she is deaf. Or she is insufferably stupid. She ran from you. Why did she run from you? "Come back!" you barked. "Come back, come back, come back!" Nothing. She just ran.

But here is your rescuer at the door. He comes to the front door and closes it behind him, then leads you back through the gate, through the backyard and into the house by the back door. Why not let you in through the front door? Why all the ceremony?

"What the hell are you doing in the front yard again?" he says, so happy to see you, and you so happy to see him, so filled with joy, so warm in the house, so much love. "You're going to end up getting picked up by the damn paddy wagon," he says. "Or worse."

Joy. Do you see how much he loves you? You do. He does not even know how much he loves you.

He does not even know how well you see it. And he does not seem to mind that you didn't catch the cat and bring her home with you. Tonight you will sleep beside his bed and protect him and She Who Sleeps Restlessly from invisible dangers. And you will sleep more soundly. As much energy is contained in the porch swing, there is far more in this room, in this bed. It warms you completely. Completely.

## K I S S

When you are on the sofa, and it's 1 a.m., and He Who Is Restless in the Night finds you there, you do not move. You pretend to sleep, but he is alert at this time of night. He sees your eyes, maybe, how they are open, and it occurs to you again. You think it occurs to you "again," but perhaps this is the first time it has occurred to you. Even if it has occurred to you before, it still feels like brand new information: you cannot see with your eyes closed.

At this thought you lift your head to see him more clearly, to allow him to see you even if it means coming down off the sofa. He does not ask you to get down from the sofa. He bends over you and touches your ears and kisses the top of your head, then moves off toward the stairway. You follow him with your open eyes. Then you step down from the sofa. You follow him to the stairs. You follow him up. Just to be near him.

## 3

# ITEMS IN AND OF THE HOUSE

The house is full of surprises. There are times when you do not recognize that there is an item in the house until it is used by one of your people, moved to a new location, or toppled over by an excited tail.

See? A lamp.

Too late.

## THE VACUUM

Do not underestimate the vacuum.

### *She Who Battles the Vacuum*

The vacuum is evil. You bark. The vacuum doesn't appear to mind you barking but you bark again. The vacuum wants to eat you and eat the sofa and eat the children. She Who Battles the Vacuum is trying to control the vacuum, but the vacuum is not in her control. It keeps moving, trying to shake free. You are not afraid of the vacuum. It is after the children. It will eat the children at its first opportunity. You bark and scare the vacuum. The vacuum is not invincible, and eventually, after it has searched every inch of the house for the children, the vacuum will give up and return to the hall closet.

### He Who Attempts to Rescue the Family

Sometimes He Who Attempts to Rescue the Family takes the vacuum out of the closet and attempts to strangle it. You know strangling the vacuum is an effort for him by the look on his face. You will help him in his struggle. The vacuum moves at odd angles and bumps its head against the wall. You think that this should hurt the vacuum in some way, that it should cry out in pain or beg for mercy. You know that if your head had been battered against the wall in this way, you would not be able to contain yourself. You do not understand the vacuum. If you were the vacuum, you would turn and bite him. But this is not the vacuum's strategy. Instead, the vacuum tries to escape. When you bark at the vacuum while He Who Attempts to Rescue the Family has a hold of the vacuum, he will yell. "Get out of my way!" he says. You don't know what this means, but you sense he is angry, and you continue to bark and pounce and snarl, positive that finally, this will be the vacuum's undoing.

### Lurking

Every time they open the hall closet, you half expect the vacuum to leap out at your people, or to leap out at you.

So you watch very carefully. You are not willing to allow them to be hurt or otherwise terrorized by the vacuum. Sometimes they will bring out the vacuum, and you think they are finally going to rid the house of this monster. It appears they are going to punish it in some way by pulling on its tail. But every time they push its tail into the two small holes in the wall, the vacuum realizes what is happening and comes to life. If there is one thing you know about your time with your people, it is this: you must, eventually, rid this house of the vacuum.

## BROOM

When the broom comes out, you jump up. Your people have complete control over the broom as it makes its way around the kitchen. Sometimes you lunge at the broom and growl, as if to say, "You may think you're menacing, but you're no vacuum."

## THE SOFA

The sofa is Position One. The sofa is a safe place. The sofa calls to you. "Sleep on me," says the sofa. But it says it slowly, in dog language, the language of sense, of comfort and good odors, of dog and person and child. The sofa makes you feel as if you are with your people even when your people are gone. So you listen. You accept. All this is yours.

### When Your People Are Away

When your people are away, you sleep on the sofa.

The sofa is a place for sleeping. You have seen He Who Sleeps on the Sofa sleeping on the sofa in the afternoon, even though he has a perfectly good bed to sleep in, so you know that the sofa is a reasonable approximation of a bed for him, and this alone means you respect the sofa as a place to sleep (even if the good odors and warmth were missing). When your people are away, and you are the only worthwhile being left in the house, you are responsible for the well-being of the household, and you must occupy Position One.

### When Your People Are Home but in the Next Room

When your people are in the next room, you sleep on the sofa. When your people come into the room, you move from the sofa to the floor and watch them carefully to see if they know you've been on the sofa. If you could speak their language, you would say, "As if!" Instead, you watch them. Do they suspect?

### When Your People Are Home and Sitting on the Sofa

When your people are sitting on the sofa, it is the perfect time to approach them, especially if there is more than one of them on the sofa. He Who Scratches Unscratchable Places will scratch your chest in the spot that is impossible for you to scratch, and you will put your ears back and squint your eyes. When he is finished, you will approach She Who Has Had Enough. She will tell you to move away. She doesn't want a stinky dog in her lap. "When did you last bathe this dog?" she says to He Who Does Not Know.

You move back and forth between the two of them because both of these responses are equally filled with the sort of adoration that fills you up like a bowl full of fresh water.

### When Your People Are Home and Lying on the Sofa

It is an especially good idea for you to approach He Who Scratches Unscratchable Places if he is in repose upon the sofa, for he is then at the perfect height for you to lick his face. Also, if you prefer, you may lick one of his hands if either is exposed. If he is not yet asleep, you may lick for several seconds before he moves his hand or turns away from you. The skin of your people is the most exotic, enticing flavor you can imagine, and you take every opportunity you can to savor it.

## TOYS

Many of the children's toys look as if they have been chewed. You don't remember doing it, but you know it was you who chewed them. This must have been a long time ago. The toys still smell like you. When you want to get the attention of Those Who Would Bathe You, you pick up one of the toys and carry it across the room and set it down in front of one of them and look into their eyes and hope they know that you love them. Sometimes your people seem to notice, and sometimes they don't. If they notice, if they take your head in their hands and scratch behind your ears and let you lick their face, it's almost as satisfying as a plate half full of leftover food on the kitchen floor, a warm place to sleep with others of your pack, a mother full of milk.

### Baby Doll

The baby doll smells of The Baby. This is your favorite toy (though it is not yours and you know it is not yours). When they are away, you will often look for the baby doll, but it is not always there, where it is supposed to be, where you left it. Sometimes The Baby moves it, or she takes it with her, and you have to settle for some other toy. You bring it into the living room and set it between your paws as you sleep. It helps you believe that one day you might be a real mother.

### Action Figures

When you pick up an action figure as if to chew it, He Who Leaps from the Furniture pounces on you and holds on to your neck and screams, "Drop it! Drop it!" When this has no effect, he lets go of you and lies on the floor, flailing his arms and legs, screaming, "She's got my Superman! She's got my Superman!" You turn and watch him and drop the toy. You do not touch it again unless he is not in the house.

*Squeaky*

The squeaky toy doesn't last long at all. Okay, you know that it's supposed to look like a hamburger, but that's not why you eat it. You know they don't really intend for you to eat it, but then why does it look (to the untrained eye) like a hamburger, and why do they give it to you if it isn't to eat and if it is going to make that awful noise? You know what a hamburger is. You've seen a hamburger. You're good with rudimentary shapes. But you're more inclined to eat dirt, really, than to eat a plastic hamburger.

So why do you eat it? It doesn't smell like food. It doesn't taste even remotely like food. When you eat it, your stomach feels as if you've eaten too much plastic (and any plastic, really, is too much plastic, especially on an empty stomach).

Why do they keep buying these? It squeaks! And when they first give it to you, and when it first squeaks, you back away from it, as if afraid it will attack—or worse, afraid all hamburgers from now on will be tasteless and small and noisy. But truly, you just wish it hadn't squeaked, because if it hadn't squeaked, you wouldn't have to eat it. But you have to make the squeaking stop. You have to keep it from squeaking ever again.

You are chewing and the toy is squeaking and you are thinking of your people, of She Who Would Feed You Plastic, and you know this is why she gives them to you, and why you eat them. This entire display of destruction is for her. She expects it of you. She keeps buying them, after all, and she must think they taste wonderful. Listen to her: "No," she says. "Oh no, not again." It is half gone. It no longer squeaks. "Why do you do that?" she says. "It's plastic, you know." What is she saying? She must think that destroying these toys pleases you. You wonder if there is a shortage of hamburger, so they give you the plastic hamburger. You want to tell her: "Enough! No more plastic hamburgers." But you can't. It would break her heart. Instead you just look at her with those eyes. You hope she understands. Their language seems so primitive.

### Black Rubber Bouncing Thing

The black rubber bouncing thing is your toy, and they let you have it inside the house. It is one of only two toys you are allowed in the house (the other is the sock toy, which began in the house so you think that is why you are allowed to have it in the house). When you drop the black rubber bouncing thing on the floor, it bounces away from you in an unpredictable direction, much as a rabbit or squirrel or other small creature might do. You love the motion of the black rubber bouncing thing more than anything else about it. You pounce on it and it bounces farther away and you pounce on it again.

Sometimes your people fill the inside of the black rubber bouncing thing with peanut butter, and you wish they wouldn't do this, because you cannot play with the black rubber bouncing thing while it smells of peanut butter. You love the peanut butter, to be sure, but you will have to lick it out completely before playing with the black rubber bouncing thing again, and you really just wanted to play with it, and if they wanted to give you peanut butter, they could have just put it on a spoon—or better yet, into a sandwich.

When you are finished licking the peanut butter out of the black rubber bouncing thing, you are too mentally exhausted to play with it. You will hide it under the sofa so they do not do this to you again.

## TABLE

That's where they eat their meals. It seems very odd the way they do it, almost as if eating is a ritual, as if eating meant more than eating. Oh, you know it is more than just eating, sure, and you will perform wonderful feats for the end of a hot dog, but they seem to elevate it to impossible heights. They worship their food. It seems wrong, but you say nothing. You simply sit nearby and wait for them to drop something. Tonight it is macaroni and cheese. You sit near The Baby.

### Table Rules

Everyone has his or her own set of table rules. The Baby is sometimes allowed on the table. He Who Leaps from the Furniture is not allowed on the table (for fear of his leaping from the table, you suppose). The cat is allowed on the table only when there is no food on the table. You are never allowed on the table. No part of your body or nose is allowed on the table. You are not allowed to lick the edges or even underneath the table. You may, however, eat all that falls from the table, so one of the best places to lie during a meal is either directly under the table or as close to the high chair as you can without anyone noticing. As soon as someone says to you, "Enough begging. Go on, go lie down," you know that they have noticed you and you are about to be put outside if you don't take action fast, so you move to the spot underneath the table that places your head near The Baby's feet.

### Leftovers

You would never ever (because they told you not to) put your front paws on the chair so that you could reach the table. He Who Cannot Keep His Chair from Tipping Over During a Meal had left his plate at the table without finishing his hot dog and tater tots, but when they all returned to find the plate licked clean, they looked at you as if they suspected you of stealing.

### Why They Suspect You

Because you did it, that's why. You are incapable of deceit. They see it in your eyes. You slink away to lie near the sofa and await persecution. When none comes, you sleep.

## S H O E S

When there is nothing to chew on, when you are bored, when it seems they are never coming home, when you know the sky is blue outside and you are stuck in the house, when the light dims and still they are not home, when it is past time to be fed, when you cannot get into the bathroom for a drink of water, when you've slept all that you can sleep for a single day, when the room is too hot and you don't know when they will be back, when you've gone to the window for the thousandth time to see if it was them, when it was not them and you cannot believe it was not them, you are dumbfounded but still expectant, and you will chew on the shoe.

There are only a few types of shoe you will chew.

The shoe must be either a sneaker or a leather shoe. Seldom are the leather shoes left out where you can get to them. You know where all the shoes are in the house, even those that are put away in the closet. You track the shoes as if they were children. When it seems you will have to chew one of them (the shoes, not the children), you select one and bring it to a comfortable but visible place in the house so that when your people come inside, they will immediately see what you have done. Sometimes you will have to move the baby doll because it is in your most favored place since that is where you have been sleeping with the baby doll between your paws. You know that what you have to do will not necessarily be a good thing, and it might cause them to roll and threaten with the newspaper, slapping it against a table or their thigh. You know what it is you are about to do and how much trouble you will be in, but you will do it anyway. You must do it. You know this the same way you know to keep track of the shoes and herd the children and check the windows for their return. If your people are lucky, they will come home before you begin. You lie with the shoe between your paws for several minutes, in almost the same position in which you were lying with the baby doll, still waiting and expecting them to come home.

Is that them?

You go upstairs to the low window with the curtain that you can push aside with your nose and you look out at the driveway and the street in front of the house.

It is not them. Whatever it was is gone now, so you return to the first floor, to your shoe.

You will be forced to chew the shoe. You sniff the inside of the shoe. It smells of He Who Would Scratch Unscratchable Places. It smells of his foot, of course. It is a pleasant odor. You test the firmness of the shoe. It is a sneaker because the leather shoes are all in the upstairs closet where you cannot get to them. This is a soft shoe. It will be good to chew on this shoe, even though it is not leather.

But that's them, isn't it? Of course! That's the sound of The Car. You should have known it wasn't them before because you always know positively when it is The Car, but you are often fooled by other cars anyway and sometimes by flying machines. The sound of The Car can wake you from sleep on the second floor of the house, in the very farthest room from where The Car enters the driveway, on the master bed, your head and paws on a pillow, dreaming of an unfriendly squirrel who visits you often in the deepest of your dreams.

Thank heaven they are home. You go to the place where you wait for them near the front window where they might see you before they come in. When they do come in, you will welcome them, circling and herding them into the house, licking a patch of skin whenever possible.

You have not chewed on the shoe. She Who Listens will explain to He Who Scratches Unscratchable Places that he shouldn't leave his shoes in the middle of the floor, that the dog will chew on them if he leaves them in the middle of the floor. He will claim that he didn't leave them there, that he put them away, that they were where they were supposed to be. He is scratching above your shoulders. You do not hear another word he says.

## CAMERA

You wish your people wouldn't aim that thing at you. It makes you think something bad is about to happen, like a lightning and thunder storm. You do not like lightning and thunder—mostly the thunder—and you do not like that thing they point at you, and you do not understand why they are so excited about the colored paper they wave in front of you after they pull it out and watch it intently for several minutes. "Wookit my shweetie widdowl buppsie— widdie wiggins woo, bupsie wupsie," they say. Sometimes their behavior is completely mystifying.

# YOU DON'T KNOW
# WHAT IT WAS

## *But You Ate It*

You don't understand what everybody is so upset about. So you ate it. Big deal. It wasn't that good anyway, and it's not as if they were going to eat it. As far as you are concerned, if they aren't going to eat it, it's yours.

## *But It Smelled of People's Feet*

And that seemed odd. It was not a shoe and it was not a sock. You know the shoes and the socks in this house. You know what they look like and you know where to find them if you need them. It almost looked like food, and it was on the table, as if being prepared for a meal. Though it smelled of their feet, it smelled too strongly of their feet, and was thus not appetizing to you. You were not tempted to eat it and you were not tempted to go much closer to it than when you first smelled it. You went closer only to confirm that this was indeed the item from which this odor was wafting. You turned away from it and walked into the kitchen, hoping someone might be slicing cheese. No one was slicing cheese, but you found a crust of bread near the oven that nobody had swept up and that you had somehow missed a half hour before when you checked the kitchen last. When you returned to the dining room, the odd-smelling item was gone. You decide it is better this way, and the event is removed from your memory.

## But It Looked Sinister

It may have been some kind of dog, though it did not bark when you barked, so you doubt it. It might also have been a lion, but did not actually move. It still may have been a lion. What you know of lions is that lions are unpredictable.

The lion did not appear at first to be furniture, though one of the children often sat on it, or picked it up and carried it from room to room, so you've come to believe that it actually was a small chair. Your people could somehow activate the lion so that it made a small and tinny roar, but they did not sit on it often because it had a tendency to tip over. Sometimes, if the children sat on the lion it would also sing a song. When the children were not sitting on the lion, it would sometimes sneak up on you and you would have to growl and bark. Oddly, it would always sneak up on you in the same place, in the corner of the dining room, just far enough away from the action of the house to be generally forgotten. For many days it sat in the living room, until everyone seemed to forget it was there. Then it was moved to one of the children's bedrooms, where it also sat unnoticed. Then it was placed in the closet, where it was apparently being punished. You always knew it was there, and you were waiting for it to come out one day, perhaps in the company of the vacuum. At first you suspected the lion and the vacuum might form an alliance, but this has never materialized.

Apparently the lion held no real ill will toward you or the children or the other people of the house, but you never trusted it, and one day, when the closet door was open, you noticed that it was gone. You have begun to believe that the vacuum ate the lion, which would confirm your suspicion that the vacuum is quite dangerous.

Dog, lion, furniture, whatever; your people are fair people and it most likely deserved whatever fate befell it.

## S O C K S

You have learned, over a long and arduous process of being told and harassed—and through repeated scolding and lessons with the newspaper and severe voices—that some socks are for playing, and others are never to be touched. Those socks that smell of you, that are tied in unusual ways so that they may never again be put on a foot, those are for playing. They are for pulling and for bringing to He Who Will Play Sock Tug. They are for setting at his feet and waiting for him to notice you there. Soon. Will it be soon?

## B E D

A bed is for sleeping. Since sleeping is very high on your list of priorities, beds are very high on your list of Important Items in the House.

*Theirs*

Only when your people are out of the house do you attempt to sleep on any of their beds. They have become aware of this somehow and will often close the doors to all the bedrooms, and at these times you are forced to sleep on the sofa. But when the door to one of the bedrooms is open, especially the door to the large, upstairs bedroom, the one that smells of a smell you smell nowhere else in the house, the one with the bathroom and the toilet to drink from (assuming the door to the bathroom is open), then you will sleep the deepest sleep you can sleep, and sometimes you hear them inside the house before you hear The Car, and you run to them. Somehow they know. You can see it in their posture, in the way they ask you, "Have you been on the bed again?"

*The Children's*

The children's beds are not as comfortable as the large and many-pillowed bed. You will resort to their beds if necessary, if the door is closed to all other comfortable places to sleep, or if they have put books and newspapers on the sofa downstairs, but you prefer not to sleep on the children's beds. The one exception to this rule—if it is indeed a rule, and you aren't always sure if a rule is a rule until the rule is broken, at which time you can be sure you will be reminded—is when one of the children is crying. Then you will go to them and crawl onto their bed as if drawn, as if magnetized, as if they are comforting you instead of you them. You are there to make certain of something. Though you don't know exactly what it is you are there to make certain of, you are certain that you must remain with them until they stop crying.

The children's tears are even saltier than their skin. You lick their faces until they push you away. Even though they push you away, you stay with them until their tears turn in to laughter, until somehow their heaving sobs become a game, until they are bouncing on the bed, in danger of hitting heads on the ceiling.

Your job is over now. You flee.

## The Children's II

The bunk bed is higher than the other beds in the house. If you scrunch yourself down, you can fit under the bunk bed. There are blankets and stuffed animals under the bunk bed because the children play under here during the day. It is a kind of hideout. It is a good hideout. When you are under the bunk bed, nobody knows where you are. Your people call for you. You let them call for awhile before revealing yourself. When you do reveal yourself, they laugh and pet you, and it is just as it should be all of the time when you are with them, when they are with you—when you are together. It is just as it often is when you greet them upon arriving home from a time away from you, only reversed. They are the ones who gather you in. They are the ones who have missed you. They are the ones who have expected you to return any moment, with just a glimmer of doubt. This is one of the ways in which they will come to understand you.

## Yours

You have your own bed. Your bed is a large pillow that your people have put on the floor for you. You will sleep there when necessary. Your bed is often more comfortable than the floor. Though sometimes you want to be closer to your people, so after they have fallen asleep, when the room is filled with the sounds and scents of sleep, you will get up from your bed and go near their bed. You will turn in a circle near their bed, scratch the carpet beside their bed as if this will make the carpet softer and more comfortable. You will sleep with your back against their bed. It helps you sleep sometimes. You will have fewer nightmares, and you will dream of empty meadows on cool, sunny days.

## Yours II

There is another bed for you in his office downstairs. He sometimes calls his office a "den," though this is like no den you have ever known. You are most comfortable in here of all the places downstairs. You are even more comfortable here than on the sofa, primarily because of his odor in here, his things on the floor and in his trash. You will sleep on your bed in his office (on which he's arranged a wool blanket), or you will sleep, sometimes, under his desk, on his feet as he sits at his desk, wiggling his toes. There is not enough room for you under his desk, but this is one of the reasons it is so very comforting to sleep there.

## CRATE

Inside, you are protected from the world. You are outside the world. You are safe and at home. You only wish you had access to the lever that opens the door. Because right now? Right now you have to pee.

## LAUNDRY

Once or twice, the laundry has come up from the basement, then was dumped on the sofa. The laundry was still warm and you buried your face in it. "Hey," said He Who Carries or She Who Sorts the Laundry (you do not remember which of them said it, though you remember them both being in the room, so perhaps it was both of them who said it), "That's clean laundry! Get away from there!" You moved away, but not before you got a good sense of why it is they take the laundry into the basement. They energize it there and make it warm. When they wear these clothes, it must make them feel invigorated all day long.

## WASTEBASKET

You try to stay out of the wastebasket. You know that you are supposed to stay out of the wastebasket, and you have made a rule for yourself never to take anything from the wastebasket. There is nothing that is strictly yours in the wastebasket, and the wastebasket is not put in the room to interest you. The things in the wastebasket will be carried

outside and dumped into a larger wastebasket and then they will be removed
from the premises on a regular sched-
ule by a giant truck with a huge
arm that apparently punishes
the large wastebasket for being
so full by flinging the waste-
basket into the air, then slamming it back to earth again.
You bark harder and louder at this truck every week, but
it continues to come.

Sometimes, once in awhile, there will be an item so
irresistible and exotic in the wastebasket that you will
ignore your rule regarding removal of items from the
wastebasket. You do not blame your people for placing
such an enticing item into the wastebasket, but they really
should have known better. They can't truly mean to throw
this item away, can they?

## TISSUE

If the tissue is new, and sitting on the floor, you will leave
it alone. If the tissue is used and sitting on the floor or on
a low table, it will be filled with enticing odors, and you
will pick it up and move it and lie down with it and pick
it apart. You will make many pieces of the tissue. You
do not eat it, exactly, but you explore it, almost scientifi-
cally, needing to discover the composition of the tissue. It
seems made of human odors. Strange and exotic human
odors.

Sometimes, if the odors are so great and unusual that you cannot resist, you will break a personal rule and pick the tissue from the wastebasket.

## T O I L E T

You drink from the toilet. You know there are other uses for the toilet, and you can smell them when you drink from the toilet. Fortunately, these are naturally occurring odors that do not concern you.

### *When It Is Encouraged by He Who Leaves the Seat Up So That You Might Drink*

Since you drink from the toilet, the children do not always see the need to refill your water bowl. So long as only He Who Leaves the Seat Up So That You Might Drink is home, this is not actually much of a problem for you.

### *When It Is Discouraged by She Who Puts the Seat Down*

The advantage of drinking from the toilet is that the water is always fresh. The disadvantage is that some of your people do not apparently want you to drink from the toilet. This confuses you, especially since they must know that the children have neglected to refill the water bowl. When water sits in your bowl for too long, it becomes stale, and you will not drink it. The toilet seems like a satisfactory alternative, until you begin to drink and She Who Puts the Seat Down begins shouting from the living room, "Did you leave the toilet seat up?" You know this means she will come into the bathroom moments from now, shooing you out and closing the lid. Even if she does this, she will not replenish fresh water in the water bowl, but will wait for the children to do it.

You must drink quickly.

## BATHTUB

This is where they bathe you. But this is also a very good place to obtain water when the toilet seat is down and the children have neglected to fill your water bowl. After someone has bathed or otherwise filled the bathtub with water, there will be droplets of water on the door runners and on the inside of the tub itself. You will have to make sure nobody is near when you lick the tub for water, as they may see you in the bathroom near the tub and think that you must want to take a bath, and this is never the case.

When there is not enough water close enough to the edge of the bathtub to drink, you will sometimes jump into the tub to lick from all sides. You must be sure that no one is in the house when you do this, for this will surely lead to a bath.

Sometimes it leads to a bath anyway. "Your feet are filthy," they say. "Look at those footprints in the bathtub." But when you resort to this and they end up giving you a bath, they somehow realize how dry your bowl must have been, and you will have fresh water more regularly for a few days. Sometimes this almost seems worth it.

## DISHES

Dishes that are placed on the floor are placed there for you to eat from and lick clean.

Dishes that are on the table or the counter are for you to ignore, but you do not ignore them. If they are low enough that you can sniff them, you may sniff them, but if your people catch you sniffing them, they will shoo you away and move the dishes somewhere else.

Dishes that are stacked into the dishwasher—even though the door is open, even though they have left the bottom rack out within your reach—are not for you to

eat from or lick. Sometimes you will find something irresistible there, such as ketchup or cheese sauce. But once again, if they catch you, you will be shooed, and most probably scolded. You will lie near the dish-washer anyway, waiting for them to forget and leave the room. Tonight they ate potatoes au gratin and corn on the cob and Polish sausage. You will take your chances.

# NEWSPAPERS

### Fetching

You have trained your people to praise you and pay closer attention to you for a short period of time after you fetch the newspaper for them. Once in awhile you will see the boy who rides past on his bicycle, delivering the newspapers. You chase him. He has more newspapers, you know it, and if you retrieved all of the newspapers he carries with him, you might be praised and petted for hours. You watch a newspaper sail onto the neighbor's porch. You fetch that one as well.

This is not encouraged.

### Punishment

The newspaper is not so much a tool of punishment as it is a tool of possible punishment. Even if they were to swat you with the newspaper, it would not really harm you. What hurts most is the scorn associated with the sound of the newspaper as they roll it up and slap it against the table or onto their hand or leg. It is like a small, targeted clap of thunder.

### Purpose for Your People

The newspaper alone is nothing to be feared. You ignore it, for the most part. You do not understand the purpose of the newspaper, but it appears to be one of the most useful and confounding tools for your people. They stare at it for long periods of time, sometimes talking to it or even yelling at it, folding it quickly and turning the pages, sometimes laughing and sometimes swearing.

When you do something they do not want you to do, such as attempt to lick a new guest in the face (you were only trying to welcome them), they will roll the newspaper up like a stick and threaten you with it.

Every day He Who Delivers the Newspaper rides past on his bicycle and tosses a newspaper onto the porch. You are a creature of ritual even more so than most creatures, and there is something about the ritual of the newspaper's arrival that makes you almost as happy as visiting friends in the country. The first few moments after the newspaper arrives are like the first kiss after a long separation. At first, only you and He Who Delivers the Newspaper know of its arrival. Only you two are aware of the difference in the universe. You savor these moments of knowledge. They are moments without time and without end.

## 4

# HEALTH AND HYGIENE

You do not think much about your own health and hygiene, and the concepts of health and hygiene are somewhat foreign to you. Instead you concentrate on getting rid of that itch even if it means biting at it until it bleeds. You consider the two states of health to be alive and dead. While you are alive, you are healthy. While you are dead, you are also healthy (in the strictly dog sense of the word), but it simply no longer matters.

Once in awhile you get the sense that your people have different definitions of *health* and *hygiene*. You don't know what these definitions are, but you sense they have something to do with the bathroom.

## THE BATH

You don't bathe yourself. Others bathe you. When you are bathed, both before and after, you get a dog biscuit. Just before you are bathed, you run away from Those Who Would Bathe You. They do not even need to go into the bathroom for you to know you are about to be bathed. They do not even need to get the shampoo out from underneath the sink. You know. And you hide. And when they call you from the bathroom door, you will come, but you will keep your head low, and you will approach them cautiously, as if readying for an ambush.

## P O S T   B A T H

What on earth is that smell? You don't want to ever smell that smell again but there is that smell and you are almost positive that it is very nearby, very close to where you are currently standing, now running, trying to escape the smell. Oh. Is it coming from you? It smells like the kitchen smells sometimes when they won't let you into the kitchen. It smells like the place you hate, though you can't remember what the place is and you don't know if you ever smelled this smell in that place, but there is that smell and it seems to be coming from your very own body, from just under your hind legs somewhere. When you seek out the smell and try to lick the smell away, instead you get the flavor of poison. This smell is poison and it is on you. You have to get it off of you. And it is on your tail. And on your back, and it seems to be coming from everywhere on your body and you have to get it off, and you go to the door and you scrape at the door, which is supposed to tell them that you need for them to open it, but they so very rarely open it quickly enough that you're sure there must be another way, so you turn circles on the linoleum every time they come close, but it seems they somehow don't notice you there, or don't know what it means when you scrape at the door and turn circles. "I'm not going to let you out," they say, "you'll just go out there and roll in the dirt." You follow them into the next room and sit near them and chew on your body hoping to get that odor, that taste, that poison off of your body. It must be eating away at your skin. It must be destroying you.

It is nearly forever before they let you out. Nearly forever. And when they let you out, you run to the grass and you relieve yourself and then you find a place in the grass and you roll onto your back and you roll onto your back and you roll and you roll as if trying to remove your own fur, your own skin. This is very nearly what you are trying to do if removing your own skin would remove the odor faster. This might be an option.

Then you go to the garden. There are expanses of dirt in the garden that you can roll in and pick up the odor of bird and cat and worm and decay. These odors will kill the poison, you think, and you roll in these odors until He Who Bathes You puts his head out the back door and screams, "Stop rolling in the damned dirt, would you?" There is anxiety in his voice and he must understand now about the poison. He must fear for your life, so you roll again. He screams again. "Get the hell in here," he screams. He must have something for you that will save you. He must know some way to kill the poison on your body, so you run into the house. But he doesn't do anything. He ignores you again. You follow him from room to room. He pours liquid into a cup and picks up a newspaper and sits in his chair. You sit near him and watch. You wait for the antidote. None comes.

You will wait. You will wait until evening. You will go outside again in the evening, if you haven't died yet from the poison, and you will roll in the garden. This is when the odor of decay is most intense anyway. In the meantime, you will lick your haunches, praying that it will not kill you.

## T H E   I T C H

That itches. You have to scratch it you have to scratch it you have to scratch it you have to scratch it. That still itches, but something is moving on the floor—an earwig? You have to eat it.

### Flea

Sometimes the itch is caused by a flea, which is a small parasitic insect that burrows into your fur and bites at you. You can feel them in your fur as they scurry and jump, scurry and jump. Sometimes you see them in the carpet, and you wonder if your people know they are in the carpet. When you see many of them, when you are always scratching at yourself to get them to leave you alone, you may hear one of your people say, "Looks like it's time to bomb the house." This usually means an overnight visit to the neighbor's.

When you return, most of the insects have disappeared from the house. What they do in here you don't know, but it somehow eliminates the insects temporarily, and makes it smell as if the air in the house has been replaced by plastic.

You wonder if your people know that these insects are also in the grass outside the house, and that they ride on your back from the yard to the house, from the house to the yard. Do they not see them out there? Do they not hear the fleas jumping from one blade of grass to the next, looking for a host, a dog or cat or squirrel?

Perhaps not. The human sense of sound, along with all other senses, appears to be quite dull.

*Mosquito*

The sound of the mosquito approaching is the most terrible flying noise to hear because by the time you hear a mosquito it is too late for you to find it in the air. It is coming close enough to land without your having the chance to nip at it, to grab it out of the air and keep it from biting you. If it lands and you do not know where it has landed, you will not know where it has landed until it is far too late, until it is taking blood from you. You are unusually sensitive to this insect taking blood from you, and it stings for a moment, then begins to itch almost immediately, and the itch will last for what seems to be years, and you will scratch at it even if it is in an unscratchable place, and you can't help but wonder if this isn't the very insect causing all the cumulative anxiety in the world.

## B R U S H I N G

You will sit still for the brushing because it pleases you to do so, though you may turn and nip at the brush and you may also not sit still at all. You may turn around to see what it is that is brushing you and you may be told to "sit still," though you do not know what this means. You will turn to see what it is that is brushing you and he will brush your head and neck and you will turn again and he will brush your back and legs and you will turn again. You will see momentarily what it is that is brushing you and though it does not appear to be of sinister intent, you will turn one more time to be sure. You will sit still when given a liver snack. You will sit still until you forget what it is that is brushing you and you will stand and turn to see what it is and turn farther, coming around to lick him in the face.

## L I C K I N G

No matter who or what you are licking, there are times when licking is a part of grooming, and other times when licking is a part of behavior, though grooming is, for you, a part of behavior, so distinguishing between the two appears to be fruitless, but you do it anyway.

You suppose that licking will get you clean, and you lick those parts of you that you can and those parts of you that are necessary to be clean, but that isn't really why you are licking those places. It just seems to be the thing you have to do when you are lying near the chair and nobody is paying close attention to you.

Also, when confused, you will sometimes turn and lick or bite your haunches, as if whatever confusion you had before licking or biting will vanish when you are finished licking or biting.

There are also times when licking is a compulsion. You just need to keep licking that spot there, and though you know it is clean and you know you've been licking it for a very long time, there is something satisfying and necessary about licking, so you lick.

There is no sense taking you to a psychiatrist. You suppose they could give you some kind of treatment for this behavior, but it is part of who you are. Why would you want to change that?

Anyway, you've only licked it red and raw once or twice.

Okay maybe four times.

Or six.

Whatever. You aren't good with mathematics.

### Yourself

You can lick yourself and you do it often, not for pleasure, really, or cleanliness, but because it nags at you, the sense that there's a part of yourself that remains unlicked. You especially need to lick yourself after Those Who Would Bathe You have just bathed you. This is how you know it is not just a cleanliness issue, since you are particularly clean at such times. Bathing seems to cause cleanliness, though it also seems to cause unpleasant odors and coldness. The world is unusually cold right after bathing.

For your people, cleanliness may, in fact, be the purpose of bathing, but you aren't sure. The purpose of bathing may also be simple wetness or punishment or even confusion on the part of your people. You have seen them bathe the children, especially when one of the children is carrying on too loudly with words such as "I'm not tired! I don't want to take a bath!"—which makes you believe that it may indeed be punishment. It may also be that when they give you a bath, you have simply been confused with one of the children, but this seems like a remote possibility. Can they not tell you apart from their own children? It's likely that they can. But they so often treat you and talk to you so much like they would treat and talk to the children that you sometimes have to wonder.

## Your People

They taste better than you do. Why do they taste so good? And furthermore, since they taste so good, why do they not lick themselves?

It must not nag at them as it nags at you. It seems to make no sense that they would not lick themselves, so when given the opportunity, when their skin is bare and you are nearby, you lick them. Some of them will tolerate this, but some of them will not. She Who Will Not Tolerate Licking will push you away and yell, "Gross. Knock it off, you stupid mutt." Whatever that means. You suspect she doesn't want you to lick her anymore, which still doesn't make any sense, so when given the opportunity, when her skin is bare and you are near, you will lick her.

You are not deterred for long, since she often leaves the tastiest parts of her skin exposed, and you do not have the willpower to stay away. You want her to know how important it is to lick the places on her body that remain unlicked, and you will lick until she pushes you away again. "Are you stupid or something? Knock it off!" It is a kind of love-tap that she gives you. A gentle nudge. You know that this is her secret joy, so in a moment, you will begin again. Her guard is about to come down. She has almost forgotten that you are nearby. There it is. You see it. A sleeveless arm.

## OBSESSIVE COMPULSIVE

Before you go out of the house, you have to stop at the door and sit, and you look behind yourself even if She Who Is About to Let You Outside is standing beside you. You look behind yourself and you face forward and you scratch at your ear, then stand and shake your head violently even though your ears have not itched in many months. They fixed your ears with the ear wash and the swabs (at least you think this is what did it—you can't think of any other reason that they would have paid so much attention to your ears except that you must have communicated with them somehow that they itched, so they found something to repair the itch so it no longer itches). If you do this long enough, scratching and shaking, she will check your ears, and though you seem to have communicated the fact that they once itched, it is apparently impossible to communicate the fact that they no longer itch (having her lift your ears and let the cold air inside can be very uncomfortable and when she does it you attempt to send her this message with the look in your eyes and a whimper that could really mean nothing else). You want to tell her that it's simply a matter of having to scratch and shake before going outside, and there's no physical reason for you to do it except for the having to do it, and maybe she doesn't operate this way. Maybe people in general don't operate this way—having to do unreasonable things in given circumstances for unreasonable or nonexistent reasons—but you cannot communicate this to her, apparently, no matter how hard you try, so you give up and submit to the inspection. When she is finished, she stands and looks at you as if she has just now discovered you in a place where you were not supposed to be.

"Nope," she says. "They look fine."

You are finished now. You can go outside. She opens the door again and you proceed slowly down the back steps. But before you go to the grassy section of the backyard to relieve yourself, you have to report to the back fence and bark three times at the dog that hasn't come outside to bark back in months. Then you have to report to the front gate and watch for the man dressed all in brown who delivers packages. You've warned your people about this man. You never know when he might come. And your people open the door indiscriminately for him and accept his packages. So you have to check for him before returning to the backyard grass to relieve yourself. Once you've relieved yourself, you repeat the process one more time, beginning with the missing backyard dog, wondering when he might come outside again, missing him in your own way and suspecting that he may never come out again, but unable to forgo the process, barking three times and waiting for his return.

## GROOMING AT THE GROOMER'S

This person. This person is the only person allowed to do what it is she does. She can somehow remove the poison from you once she has put it on. She can somehow make a hot day seem cool. She can somehow leave you feeling lighter. She makes noises about your head and neck and buttocks that concern you, but you never come to any harm, and you have no inclination to hurt her. When you are away from her, you long for her as you might long for a cousin you see on occasion. An old friend. You will be lighter when you are finished with the groomer, ready to meet the world nose to nose. She is a lover. She smells of apples.

## T H E   P I L L

You are not going to eat that. What is it? It's white. And so small. It can't be food. There is no edible food that is white. Except white bread.

You love white bread.

Whatever that is, you aren't going to eat it. Anyway, it isn't enough to fill you up even if it was food. If you ate it, you would still be hungry. But it isn't food and it isn't an insect. It doesn't even move. Insects move. Unless they are curled up hiding from you like a roly-poly bug. But roly-poly bugs are vile and inedible and anyway they don't move fast enough for you to notice them so you don't eat them.

Your people can put it in your mouth and rub your throat all they want, but you aren't going to eat it. No way. They've tried this before and when they were finished, you simply rolled it out from the back of your throat and dropped it on the kitchen floor.

Oh, and sure, of course, you'd much rather have that peanut butter sandwich anyway. Now that you'll eat. What were they thinking? That tiny nugget of nonfood or the peanut butter sandwich on the white bread (the only really good white food, and it is so very good) with the big glob of peanut butter in the middle. Is that even a choice you should have to make? Can they not make this choice for you?

You wonder what they're going to do with the white thing now that they have given up trying to feed it to you. You don't see it anywhere and maybe they ate it themselves. You would have to eat a lot of those if you didn't want to be hungry anymore.

Your people are sometimes the most ridiculous people you know.

## EAR WASH

Nope. You will not hold still for this. You've held still one too many times for this. Yes, just that once was one too many times. He Who Makes You Sit Before He Touches You is trying to fill up your ear with liquid, just as She Who Stings Your Hip has done. He's cooing, trying to make the sound of a bird, it seems, and this sound irritates you. If he does manage to get some of the liquid into your ear, it sounds like you've got the ocean inside your head. You know this is supposed to do something for you, but you barely believe it could be true. It's the ocean right there in your head!

Of course you know what the ocean sounds like. You've seen the ocean. Or anyway a friend of yours has seen the ocean and you smelled it on her when she came back from the ocean. What else do you need to know? It smelled of a great and powerful liquid sound.

You are stronger than your people, so when they try to put the ocean in your ear, you can easily pull away from them. And when they call you back, you have no fear that they will be able to hold you this time, so you go back to them and let them try again.

Especially now that they've put the bottle away and

they have a dish full of cotton balls. You have no fear of the ocean, and He Who Makes You Sit Before He Touches You makes you sit, then he kneels near you.

You will hold still and find out what it is that's going to happen, and he presses something into your ear, and then he rubs, and this is nothing like the ocean now. He rubs much as She Who Stings Your Hip rubbed your ear. You wonder if this has anything to do with the itching that is gone now and has been gone for so very long. He rubs your ear and—Oh—that feels good. Mm. You were going to pull away, but you can't remember what from.

There is the ocean again, though you hardly notice it now. Why is it that it sounds like the ocean inside your ear when all he is doing is rubbing?

You've got to shake the ocean out of your ears. Shake it right the heck out.

"Not over here!" he screams. "Over there!" he points. You don't know what he's saying. All you hear is your ears flapping and the ocean removing itself into the air.

## GERIATRIC

As you grow older, you will spend more time wondering about the noises and pains of your body, both major and minor. As you grow older, you will become more dependent upon your people, and they will spend more time attending to your health, like this:

You have been up for a few minutes, or a few hours, or you didn't sleep all night.

Your littermates would know. But your people are not littermates, are they? No. You have to remind yourself of this. They are friends. They live here and you would sleep with them but it is too difficult to get up onto the bed, and anyway they sometimes move in the night and wake you and then it takes you too long to fall back asleep and then you will be up.

There she is. She Who Would Welcome You with Warm Sounds. Her sounds are warm. You adore her sounds. They are like a balm. They calm you somehow, but as she approaches, the reality of your love and anticipation is too strong and you begin to circle and circle and hope and hope that she will come closer and bend down and touch or pick you up or just love you back.

She's standing now and not approaching and you wonder what is wrong and you turn more quickly so she will know how urgent it is. You wonder what it is that has made her stop and then you don't wonder anymore when you release your bladder onto the floor and she lets out a soothing sigh like this one: "Oh, no. Why every morning? What do I have to do?" You remember this now. You did this yesterday. Yes. You will try to remind yourself for tomorrow, won't you? You'll remember for tomorrow. You think you might have done this one or two times before. Or more. You don't know. You remember clearly but it seems as if maybe it was all on one day, it all happened just this once, just today, here on the floor.

She's on her hands and knees with a cloth. What is she cleaning? What has happened? Why aren't you going outside? Doesn't she know that if she doesn't hurry up you might relieve yourself on the floor? You have a sense of having done this maybe once or twice before, unable to control your bladder. Or imagining it, wondering what would happen if you actually did it.

Then she is finished and she gives you your magic peanut butter cracker. When you have your peanut butter cracker, your day will change.

Then you go for your walk. You smell all the smells of the neighborhood, and you smell them as if they are all new. And though you have to relieve yourself and you do so in all the regular places, the urgency with which you have to relieve yourself is quite small, and you are surprised by its smallness, as you generally have to relieve yourself rather urgently first thing in the morning.

You hope you are not ill.

But by the end of your walk you feel the effects of your peanut butter cracker. Already it is smoothing out the edges. It makes life seem so much richer and more complete, less complex and confusing. It makes your life seem fuller and richer. Generally more casual. It is a brilliant, magic cracker.

As you re-enter the house, you are greeted by your housemates, by your nonlittermates. This greeting doesn't bother you as you remember it bothering you so often before. You let them greet you and you continue on toward your bed. You are feeling so sleepy now. You just want to put your head down for awhile. It has been so long since you remember sleeping. Your morning nearly over. Thank God you're finally home.

## 5

# FRIENDS AND RELATIONS

You have many friends and relations. Your relationships with them are unqualified. You pour yourself into their lives as if they are vessels for your emotions, for you. It is possible that they are vessels not quite large enough to contain you. But you keep pouring anyway.

### FAMILY

Your family is determined by time, not by birth. You spend your time with this family, with this group of people—Those Who Would Bathe You—and because you have grown up with them and because you live with them and because you love them more dearly than your own life, they are your family.

Do not be mistaken. You remember your birth mother, and she is as much family as your people, but she is distant, and you recognize that this distance has caused you to romanticize her, to separate from her even in your romance. Your birth mother has become memory. Sometimes you remember her as she is, as a mother with milk and care and disregard for all things unnecessary to the nourishment of her pups. Other times you remember her in the most primitive, nonsensical way—she becomes home, and you long for her. This is usually at night. You try to wake yourself, but you are already awake.

## B A B Y   L O V E

You love the baby. The baby drops food on the floor. The baby is your favorite of all of Those Who Would Bathe You. The baby, though she is one of Those Who Would Bathe You, has never bathed you.

The baby is as much your baby as she is their baby. Though a human baby, she is yours. You have spent all her life loving her.

## O T H E R   C H I L D R E N

There are some children who would torture you. You love even these children unless they are outside the gate. If the gate is closed, you will bark at them to let them know the house is not their house, the gate is not their gate, the yard is not their yard. If the gate is open, you will sit at the gate and watch them pass, sure that if you were to bark now they would be confused. Humans are easily confused.

## C I R C L E

You love all Those Who Would Bathe You not because they would bathe you but because they are not only Those

Who Would Bathe You but also Those Who Would Put Their Plate on the Kitchen Floor After They Are Finished or Nearly Finished. Those Who Would Put Their Plate on the Floor After They Are Finished or Nearly Finished are also Those Who Would Touch and Pet You. Those Who Would Touch and Pet You are also Those Who Would Throw the Ball or the Frisbee or the Black Rubber Bouncing Thing. Those Who Would Throw the Ball or the Frisbee or the Black Rubber Bouncing Thing are also Those Who Would Let You Up on the Bed If There Is No One Else in the House to Comfort Them. Those Who Would Let You Up on the Bed If There Is No One Else in the House to Comfort Them are also Those Who Would Take You for a Ride in the Car and Roll Down the Window for You to Stick Your Head Out. Those Who Would Take You for a Ride in the Car and Roll Down the Window for You to Stick Your Head Out are also Those Who Would Take You Through the Drive-Through, Who Would Order a Happy Meal Just for You, and Let You Eat It in the Front Seat with Them. Sometimes Those Who Would Bathe You let you lick them in the face and the circle is complete.

## NEIGHBOR

The neighbor is second only to your people as far as favorite people go. The male neighbor—He Who Bites Your Ears—grabs a hold of your ears and puts his face in your face. Sometimes he nips your ears and it reminds you of something so deep in your stomach that it aches. This is a different kind of love than the love you feel for your people. But it is a kind of love and you recognize it as such. When he comes close, especially if he takes you by surprise, you kneel down and wait for him, and he never fails to approach, and he never fails to call you a "worthless hound," which you know he means so strongly that you love him more and differently each time you see him. "What a dog," he says. "What a worthless dog." If it weren't for your people, you would follow this man anywhere.

## R O M A N T I C   M E M O R Y

Your romantic memory of your mother goes like this:

You remember your mother fondly. You remember suckling. You remember your brothers and sisters. You remember biting them and you remember them biting you. You remember being picked up by the scruff of the neck. You haven't seen your mother in years. You miss her terribly. You remember her as you remember the rest of them, your brothers and sisters. By scent. You haven't smelled that exact smell since then, but you remember, and when it seems you smell them, when there is a scent that reminds you of them, when the sun is as high as the sun ever gets and the grass is tall enough to reach your belly, when the wind is just strong enough to make you remember your ears and the joyous sound of the wind, that's when you smell the smell that smells something like them.

They smell like heaven.

## PACK

You've never been Alpha but you've never been Gamma, either. You don't know if there is a Gamma, but you take satisfaction in the knowledge that you've never been Gamma, even if there is no such thing as Gamma. Those Who Would Bathe You are almost always Alpha, though sometimes they don't know this. All they need do is ask and they are Alpha.

While they are away, in different parts of the city, in different parts of the world, and while you are at home, alone, near the gate and waiting for them to return, that's when you are Alpha. There is little comfort in it. As soon as they come home, you will abandon this antiquated hierarchy. Good riddance.

## BIG BLACK DOGS

Those big black dogs walk past the window with their people every day and you must bark at them. They are big and black and you are hoping one day one of the two of them will at least look at you because you are barking, but they don't even seem to notice that you are making one giant racket and moving from one end of the sofa to the other trying desperately to get their attention and now you've fallen. You've fallen off the sofa. You are going to stay down here. You are going to lie beside the sofa and hope nobody noticed. Not the two big black dogs and certainly not your people. You have done this before. Perhaps you will do this again tomorrow. For now, it is enough that you lie here and forget.

## Y O U   A N D   O T H E R   S P E C I E S

You are somewhat familiar with, or have had some kind of relationship with, the following incomplete list of animal and insect species:

### Squirrels

You do not dislike squirrels, but you are attracted by their motion. They are very fast. If they are outside your fence, you bark at them. You will continue to bark at them even if it seems they have left the area, for you know the squirrels have never really left the area. They are always close by. That tree in the backyard. That is a home for squirrels. You know they are there. You know it.

When they move, you feel your whole body thrust forward as if it is moving without you. You cannot stop yourself. All you know is chase. All you know is Squirrel Quickly Running. All you know is Must Catch Squirrel. You run and run and run, and it flies up a tree. Yes, it seems to fly. How does it fly? You wish you could do that. You really wish you could do that. You bark at the tree, but the squirrel will not come down. He's out on a branch now, as if oblivious of you. He looks at you, looks away. He looks at you, looks away.

You have never caught a squirrel, and you don't know what you would do with one if you did catch him. You imagine that you would pick him up in your mouth the way you pick up the tennis ball. But then where would you put him? Also, you imagine he would bite and scratch you, but you know you would have no control over what would happen if you caught the squirrel, so you don't worry about it. Your body would know what to do with a squirrel if you ever caught a squirrel. You simply do not worry. Very little causes you to worry. Some days you think that there is no such thing as worry. You don't remember the last time you worried. You have a feeling that you did worry one time, but you don't remember what about.

Quite possibly it was about when your people were coming home. This seems right, but it was so long ago that they left, you don't remember if it was worry or even if such a thing exists.

The squirrel does not seem worried about you either, and for good reason. You mean the squirrel no harm.

### Rabbits

You have seen rabbits in the garden, but you never see them for long. You would not bother chasing them except that before you even know they are rabbits you are running toward them at top speed, thinking maybe they are squirrels or even cats (not your cats, of course, but other cats) and you continue to chase them even after you know they are rabbits because you're supposed to chase them, aren't you?

If you are lucky, the gate to the garden will be open. If you are unlucky, you will attempt to charge through the wire fence at near full speed. You know that this fence is there, and you know it would be easy to avoid at a slower speed, but you are so focused on the rabbit that you cannot be bothered by the hindrance of a fence or other barrier until it is too late.

He Who Built the Fence and the Gate to Keep You Out of the Tomatoes is doubled over with laughter, convulsing in what looks more like pain. "You stupid dog," he says, and you go to him after you have given up on the rabbit. You sit before him and hope his pain will subside. When it does, he rubs you on the head and behind your ears. "You okay, pup?" he says. "Gotta take it easy there, okay?" Apparently he is okay. And thank goodness. You don't know what you would do if he became suddenly ill. Something drastic, you are sure.

You can't decide why your face hurts. Your memory of such things is always rather vague.

### Skunk

Though it seems you are about to encounter an interesting and knowledgeable creature, one you are willing to get to know better and find out more about the world from, the skunk apparently does not appreciate your approach.

Nor do your people appreciate your having returned to the house with the skunk's endearing—and enduring—odor on your body. Your people react oddly, though. They bathe you with some kind of delicious food. You wish this is how they always bathed you. How can you communicate this desire to them?

Perhaps the skunk will return. You have much to share with her. For instance, has she seen the dogs that used to live in the house behind your house? Does she know what has happened to them?

### Porcupine

You have encountered only one porcupine in your life. You recognize them now. It will be your last encounter. Or so you hope.

### Deer

You have seen deer from the car or when visiting other places, other dogs. Many dogs tell you of deer, of chasing deer or being in the company of deer. Deer seem almost intelligent, and you would never chase or bark at them. You actually saw what you thought was a deer last week in the yard behind your yard, where your friends used to live, but when you came closer, he moved off into the fog. You did not bark at him, thinking it was a deer and, as you have noted, you would never chase or bark at a deer.

This is not a matter of principle, but one of respect. You have no need to chase or bark at deer, especially the most intelligent and stately of them. You also do not wish to be gored through the stomach by a male deer that you might mistake for a female deer. The stories you've heard of this happening are so graphic that some of them must be true, and you are pretty sure if it was going to happen to anybody chasing a male deer, it would happen to you chasing a male deer.

## Phantoms

Your people do not seem to have any kind of relationship with or knowledge of phantoms. You are not sure yourself if they even exist. There are times when you must bite or chase or stomp, quite sure that there had been something there to bite or chase or stomp a second ago, and your people act as if you've gone mad. You did not see anything, exactly, but the biting and chasing and stomping satisfied your need to rid the room of something you were quite sure was there. Perhaps you are not protecting your people from phantoms so much as you are chasing air. If there is something there, and you chase it away, then you have done a good thing for your people. If there is nothing there, however, then you have done no harm. You sometimes sense that, at the very least, your antics are entertaining to your people.

## KITTEN LOVE

Though you will chase cats from the yard and you will bound across the street to remove them from your sight and though you will bark at them from behind the gate until your bark is hoarse and almost vanished, you love the kitten.

### New Kitten

What did they do?

Look at her! She's impossible to clean. Her fur is too fine. Her claws too quick to strike. Settle down, furball!

That's your tail. *Leave it.* That's your tail. *Leave it.* That's your paw. *Leave it.* Your nose. *Leave it!*

You will lick her. You will put your paw on her back and lick between her ears. That's what you'll do, and you won't stop until she's learned who is boss.

That's your nose! *Ouch!*

Curious, odd, crazy, how much you can love her, how much you want her to be happy, to love you back, to leap on your paw or your tail and hold on, no matter how much it hurts. Curious how you want her love almost more than you want your people's love. How can that be so? What is different about her? Why will she come closer only when you want to be left alone?

### Teaching the Kitten

She does not listen to you. You've told her about getting up on the table and you've told her about being on the furniture (though your people apparently have slightly different rules for the kitten, because they don't even seem to notice that she's on the sofa unless she is also digging her claws into it in an apparent attempt to pull it to pieces), and now this.

You've come in from outside and she's in the dining room with one of the socks that is not for chewing and she is chewing it, batting it, and tossing it, and rather than attempt to get the kitten's attention long enough to teach her a lesson, you simply dash into the dining room and take it from her, grabbing a hold with your teeth and removing it from her mouth before she has even noticed you are in the house. It has been an exquisitely long time since you've had one of the socks that are not to be chewed in your mouth, and you take it into the living room with you and do a quick mental calculation of how long you will be able to hold on to the sock before someone notices that you have it, and you calculate again, wondering if you might hold it on the floor with your paw for a moment and give it a tug, but instead you turn and watch the kitten for a reaction and drop the sock at your feet.

She apparently cannot understand what has just happened. She sits for awhile in the center of the dining room, near the table, allowing time to pass. This is unlike her. You wonder if you have hurt her feelings, so you approach, only to find that she is unapproachable. She backs away, then swats at your nose, then sails up and onto the chair, then up and over your head, onto your shoulders where she bounds off somewhere behind you. You look back just in time to see her picking up the sock in her mouth and carrying it off, the proud hunter. Fine enough, you suppose. Let her learn this lesson on her own. A lesson learned the hard way is better learned, yes?

When you turn your attention back to your people, you find them doubled over either in pain or laughter. It sounds like laughter. Whatever it was that has caused this outburst of laughter has clearly finished. You don't see anything anywhere that would cause such an event. You are sorry that you missed it.

### Kitten Indifference

Another one? Is this one staying too?

Alas.

### Kitten Confusion

What is this thing? Why does she do that? Where did she come from? Why am I not allowed to chew on her neck?

And why, then, is she allowed to chew on me?

### Kitten Primacy

They are your people. You will put your face in He Who Holds Mewling Cat's Face until he recognizes that you were here first, until he recognizes that you are far cuter than any feline, until he recognizes that he loves you, that he has always loved you, that your love has no end, and that the kitten will one day be nothing more than a cat . . . a cat who only demands and never gives. You give. You give and give and give. You are giving right now. What is the kitten giving? You want to ask him in human language: "What is this kitten giving you right now?" But then you don't want to ask. You think better of that question. You are afraid of the answer.

## CAT POWERS

Why does the cat get to go out the front door? What have you done? You will not cross the street, which the cat does. You will not dig in the neighbor's garden, which the cat does. You will not walk along the top of the fence, which the cat does. And by the way, how does she do that? Her powers are extraordinary.

You do not envy her.

You do not.

## BIRD

It wasn't your fault. You loved the damn bird (as you love most animals). You loved to sit and listen to him talk his stupid language. It was a stupid language, but it had its appeal too. He Who Tries to Speak the Bird's Language let the damn thing out of its cage. You just did what you do. It flies past your nose—so very close, motion upon motion spinning wildly in on itself as a flying bird will fly, blue and chaotic and remarkable—it flies, and you simply do what you, a dog, must do.

You must pluck it from the air, that's what.

Exactly.

## WHY YOU STAY

There are times when you know perfectly well that you could leave and never come back here. You can escape this gate easily enough. You can jump the fence. You can simply leave when the front door is left open, if you want. But you don't, and though you don't often question your reasons, you sometimes list them for yourself, not because you need to be reminded of them, but simply because you can't help yourself.

### Reason 1

They will eventually drop food on the floor.

### Reason 2

Closely related to Reason 1, they will often place food on the floor for you to eat. This is not an accidental meal, but a meal given with purpose. They care for you, even though they are not dogs. You suspect that they must use reason and have ethical standards, just like you.

### Reason 3

Closely related to Reason 2, they sometimes bring home a bag of the expensive dog food. This comes relatively close to resembling the food they might drop on the floor, which is what you really want to eat. Sometimes they also drop food onto the floor, or He Who Feeds You What He Will Not Eat Himself will toss cheese from the kitchen counter for you to catch, or otherwise drop the cheese onto the floor, but these really belong within Reason 1. That they feed you anything at all proves to you that they are ethical beings, though you suppose some dogs might argue this point. You will not. You believe in your people.

*Reason 4*

Despite their idiosyncrasies and their tendency to slide their feet under your belly as you sleep, you care for your people, and you would miss them if you decided to leave.

*Reason 5*

You would ask anyone who demanded such a ridiculous list: "Ever slept outside, during the winter, under a bush?" They would shrug. They would indicate that they had not done this with some gesture. "No," they might say. "Have you?"

You haven't. But you have the good sense to know that it can't be as warm outside as being curled up against the legs of She Who Makes Room on the Bed After He Has Fallen Asleep. It makes good sense to you to avoid finding out for sure.

## L A N G U A G E

Language appears to be a selfish matter within species. In general, no two species share exactly the same language. Within a given species, the language may vary just enough so that it can be difficult to understand even those within your own species. For instance, some of the smaller variations of dog appear to have body language that a larger dog cannot duplicate or understand without a great deal of difficulty.

Some extremely small dogs appear to vibrate or quake, and you do not always know if they are attempting to communicate or if their nervous system has simply gone haywire. You suspect the latter, but based on human response to this vibration, you also believe that these small dogs have developed a method by which they communicate information to humans without the humans actually having to speak any of the dog language. You do not understand how this is possible, but you simply observe that when a small dog begins to vibrate, the human species reacts to that vibration in a positive manner, one that you cannot apparently duplicate. You do not know what is being communicated, and you understand the communication is not intended for you, so it doesn't matter, really, that you don't understand it. You simply observe with a kind of unpleasant jealousy. You wish for a moment that you could do that. But when you try, it makes your bones ache. You will leave it to the smaller dogs. Perhaps it is compensation for being too short to reach the toilet and therefore having to drink from a bowl set on the floor, and therefore having to rely on humans to remember and refill it.

### Human Replication

Why does he do that? He makes the high-pitched whining noise and he looks at you. And you don't have a choice, really. Though he's not howling in the traditional dog sense . . . though he's not accurately portraying a midnight message—or even a daytime message, for that matter—you cannot control the

urge to reply. He will not understand what you're telling him, of course, but he is entertained by your response. He gets some pleasure out of it. He will think that he has communicated with you, and in some sense this is true. He has said: "I wish I could say something to you in your own language." You want to tell him that it isn't that simple, and sometimes you try to say this to him, but what you end up saying is, "I wish I could communicate with you in your own language." You know very little interspecies language other than nonverbal communication. You have tried everything on him, but he doesn't seem to understand you. You imagine there is some way to make him understand, but you are not likely to find out what it is during your lifetime.

### Cat

You speak a very small amount of cat. Or rather, you understand a small amount of their language, but it also seems that perhaps cats have a very limited vocabulary, especially when compared to dogs. You know that when a cat makes the small enginelike noise, she is generally content. You know that when she arches her back, she is warning you against putting your nose near her genitals. When she runs away from you and leaps onto the back of the sofa and looks away from you, this is when she is seeking love, and this is when you love her the most.

## 6

# EAT AND DRINK

If humanity has a higher purpose, you have decided that this higher purpose must be to feed you. It will be enough for them in the end that they have supplied you with enough to eat, with a replenished water supply and leftover goulash. It will be enough, in the end, that they have served you, and you believe in your deepest heart of hearts that feeding you is its own reward.

## MEALTIME

The children are supposed to feed you. They are forgetful. They forget to feed you. Their parents remind them, but sometimes they still forget to feed you so you prompt them by standing at the kitchen door, touching the doorknob with your nose periodically, hoping they will understand the urgency of the matter. When you do this, She Who Sometimes Feeds You When the Children Forget might turn to you and open the door to the mudroom, then open the screen door to let you out. You look outside. You do not want to go outside. You do not go outside. You look at the bowl. She says something that sounds

like, "I'm not going to feed you. The children feed you."
You are hoping she will send in the children to feed you.
You hope she will remind the children. Eventually, the
children will cease whatever it is they are doing and come
to the mudroom and feed you. It occurs to you every time
that the children are not very well trained. But you
remember yourself as a puppy. You do not judge them.


## BREAKFAST

When is breakfast? How do you know when it's time for
breakfast?

When there is food nearby and the day is new, then it
is time for breakfast. Or when you remember that you
should be eating soon and you're pretty sure if you go to
the back door and beg, you'll get fed even if nobody in
the house is awake yet, then it's time for breakfast. Or even
when you've just discovered, again before anybody is
awake, that they left three slices of half-eaten garlic bread
and four crusts (the children do not eat their crusts) out on
the kitchen counter, then it is exactly time for breakfast.


## LUNCH

What do you prefer for lunch?

Cheese tossed to you as you wait, as your people prepare sandwiches. Also bologna, salami, turkey, liverwurst,
chicken fat, brisket of beef, bread crusts, apple peels, apple
cores, carrot sticks, half peanut butter sandwiches on white

bread, potato chips, hot dogs, pretzels, bagels with cream cheese, string cheese, and Cheez-It brand crackers. But no olives, thank you very much. They can keep those for themselves. They are not edible. You don't know why they eat them. You are quite certain that olives are poisonous, and you wish you could prevent your people somehow from eating them. They will die from eating them some day. Then you will be alone.

## SUPPERTIME

When is it suppertime?

When there is food available. In reach. Any time of day that you weren't already eating. The food doesn't necessarily have to be intended for you, especially when your people are not in the house and when they have neglected to feed you before they left (in this way, suppertime is much like breakfast and relies heavily on opportunity). Sometimes, when they leave, you have been known to stand on your hind legs and lick a plate clean of pork fat before your people have even pulled out of the driveway. Once in a while they have even returned to the house to find you this way, shocked and surprised and loving you all the more. They left the plate so near the edge of the counter. They know it is their own fault. Sometimes, right then, they fill your bowl with food. Had the bowl been filled with

food in the first place, you would have eaten the pork fat anyway. Honestly, it was so very near the edge of the counter.

## STEAK

You don't know what it is about steak, but you sense it before it is possible to sense it, and when its odors fill the air, you do nothing but salivate and sit as close as possible to He or She Who Sears the Steak, until they tell you to move away, at which point you move closer. They will not give you any of this steak until much later, until after they have devoured most of it, and you know this, but you cannot help but be so close. It is almost as if you are eating it. That is how close you are. That is how present the steak is in your mind. Nothing else matters. Not even the slippery linoleum in the kitchen. You won't fall. If you were judged based on this time alone, you would be judged lower than an animal. You would be simple desire. Perhaps you shouldn't have your paws up on the counter like this. You don't remember if there was a rule. The odor of steak, the plate full of meat—who can think of anything else when there is steak?

## NEW DOG FOOD

What is this? Is this supposed to be food? You will not eat this. You turn up your nose at this. If you knew what a hunger strike was, you would go on a hunger strike. You would let yourself get very hungry and very skinny. You would let your rib cage show. That's how skinny you would be. You would be in danger; you would be so thin.

You would lie on a mat and drink water through a straw. You would tell people that as soon as they brought back your old dog food for you, you would eat it.

You pace the kitchen floor, waiting for your old dog food to be returned to your old bowl.

"Come on now," they say. "I spent an extra five bucks on that food." Apparently they see your dismay. They understand and have decided to give you your old food. Except they don't go and get the old food. They leave this new food in the bowl. And you are getting hungrier. You suppose that your ribs might be showing right now. You feel sorry for She Who Fed You Though Usually She Doesn't. She is probably feeling guilty that she gave you this new food that you will not eat. She is feeling guilty that your health is at risk because you will not eat. She can see your rib cage and is worried and is maybe going to call She Who Stings Your Hip right now, making an appointment to bring you in for a new stinging of your hip or ear washing or other painful or unusual treatment.

Your hunger strike might as well be over. You proved your point. No sense torturing her.

Hey, this stuff isn't half bad.

## CAT FOOD

Sometimes they leave you no choice but to eat the cat food. How long has it been since they were supposed to feed you? Has it been five minutes already? It isn't your fault. You couldn't wait any longer.

And the cat food is vile. It is worse than eating raisins. Worse, even, than cashews.

Okay, maybe not that bad. But at least as bad as raisins.

## P I Z Z A

As it is for many of the carnivorous species, pizza is very nearly your favorite food. There is something about pizza, about the combination of fats and carbohydrates and sauces. There is something about pizza.

Unless it is pizza with olives. But if it is pizza with olives, it is still salvageable. You will then eat the pizza, taking care to eat none of the olives. You do not have the skill to remove the olives first, as you have seen the children do, but you can manage to spit them out before they enter your body in any significant way. Once The Baby dropped an entire slice of olive and mushroom pizza on the floor. Since you were nearby, you rescued the slice and devoured it in moments. You have become very good at holding the olives inside your mouth when devouring pizza. You leave a small pile of olives on the floor. When you are finished, your people say, "You've got to be kidding me. How did you eat that without eating the olives?" They must be catching on. Perhaps one day they will have the same aversion to olives as you. You will teach them. Someday.

## MOTHER'S MILK

What does your mother's milk taste like? Do you remember? You have a strong recollection of it. Your recollection tells you that it doesn't matter what it tasted like. That it tasted like nothing and everything. It was the only thing. Why ask such a question? In those days, in those very early days, it was simply all there was in the world, and it was more than just food. It was your mother imprinting emotional memory upon you. And it was more even than that somehow. Does anyone understand that? Do you?

## RAWHIDE BONE

 Once in awhile, they give you a rawhide bone. You will chew it and eat it as quickly as possible. Unless there is nobody home. If there is nobody home, you prefer to wait until one of your people is in the room with you, especially the one who gave you the rawhide bone. You will sit near She Who Gave You the Rawhide Bone and chew on it until it is soft and lovely. She Who Gave You the Rawhide Bone will eventually take the rawhide bone and move it into the mudroom and close the door. "This is disgusting," she says. You don't know what this means, but you feel she must be terribly pleased with you. You will not touch the rawhide bone again until desperate for this same loving affection. Then you will bring it inside and set it at her feet

and chew it. "Gross," she says. "That is so disgusting." Yes. She must be very pleased indeed.

## PEPPERONI

You have tricked He Who Would Eat Pepperoni When He's Alone in the House into giving you substantial portions of the pepperoni by following him from room to room, sitting near him when he sits, and looking at him as if you will tell all when She Who Sometimes Finds Out gets home. He should know that there was some purpose for the pepperoni (most probably pizza) or there wouldn't be pepperoni in the house in the first place, and he should also know that she is going to discover that the pepperoni is missing anyway and know exactly who it was who ate it, but he falls for your rhetorical device regardless and feeds you as he eats and watches through the front window for her car to return from wherever it has been. It is at times like these that he reminds you most of yourself, and you are glad that this was his idea and not yours.

You are also glad that you cannot open the refrigerator. If you could open the refrigerator, there would be one feast to remember, then there would be no end to the amount of trouble you would be in.

## CHOCOLATE

An entire plate of food that makes your head spin, that makes you drunk and feel as if you've just found your mate hiding in the closet of your own house, as if he'd been there all along, as if he'd taken the shape of the vacuum to observe your behavior and was only now satisfied that you would do nicely and was therefore revealing himself to you. It feels dangerous somehow, but you devour the entire plate full of gorgeous love, wrappers and all (you have never been good with removing wrappers without eating at least some of the wrapper along with the food contained inside).

When you are finished, you lie near the back door, relatively sure that your people will be home soon.

When it becomes an emergency to do so, you go to the middle of the living room to do it. Even the wrappers are there. The chocolate and wrappers upchucked onto the floor. This seems like such a waste that sometimes you eat a portion of it a second time. Just enough to defray the waste. Then you lie on the sofa and wait for them to discover what has happened. There is no sense avoiding the sofa. When they discover what has happened, they will speak to you with every tone available to them, then they will put an arm around you and stroke your head and shoulders. This is good enough reason to have done what you have done. Though you feel a little sick, this has happened often enough for you to know that it will soon pass. It will turn out to be the best thing for everyone.

## CHEESE

Can you imagine a more delicious and versatile human food? When cheese is being prepared in the house, you make sure that you are near the cutting board. Your people use cheese in their meals almost every day, and almost every day at least a small portion of the cheese will drop to the floor, whether it be by accident or on purpose. And whether it is by accident or on purpose, it really doesn't matter. So long as it is within reach.

## PEANUT BUTTER

This stuff is fabulouth, but you with, uh, mmm, you with, you, uchelm, ith, ickuld, ishn't sho stucki in thu ruff off yoor mooth. Thoory. Juth a minnuth.

Othay.

There.

It'th very thticky stuff. It thometimeth taketh dayth before you feel yourthelf again.

## HOT DOG

What was that? It was magical. It was the most wonderful thing you can imagine. It was like the culinary equivalent of paradise. You hope that there are more such things in the world. So salty and meaty and soft and easily swallowed and quickly consumed. What was it? What is it called? You call it Tube of Meat, and suppose they must have some similar name for it. Or they call it Treasured Food, or Consummation of Desire, or Perfect. Simply perfect. They wrap it so pleasantly for themselves, it must be a truly special food, and you will be grateful for yours, and you will sit closer, waiting to see if there is another coming your way.

## NONFOOD ITEMS YOU MIGHT HAVE TO EAT

Sometimes you are forced, by instinct or desire or impulse, to eat items that would not otherwise be considered food. Or should not otherwise be considered food. You suppose someone might consider them food. You hope this doesn't offend anybody. If it is food, you don't want it to be your food. That's all.

### Insects

If you do not eat the insects, they will only grow and become more menacing. Some of them will grow to the size of large cats, and this is the least desirable size for almost any living creature.

### Flies

Though they do not taste like anything edible you have ever eaten before, they move exactly like something that should be edible, so you eat them. Sometimes you will leave them dying in the carpet and swat at them with your paw, at which time they cease to be edible. Now they are a plaything. You are disappointed when they finally stop moving. You have lost your plaything. Perhaps you will eat one now and then, but they are not yummy at all. They taste like medicine.

## Wasps

Yes, you have eaten wasps. Yes, they have stung the inside of your mouth. Given the opportunity, you will do it again anyway. The sting is not so painful as the joy of conquest.

## Mosquitoes

You leave mosquitoes alone if they are in the air because they are too hard to catch. But if they are biting you in a place where your tongue can reach them, you will eat them. They taste like raw meat. This does not exactly make sense to you, since they are the smallest of the insects that you will eat, but they do, indeed, taste like a steak, like a tiny cut from the best part of a much larger beast.

## Spiders

Your relationship with spiders is entirely reactionary. You will eat spiders, but only because they move along the floor or wall, not because they taste good or because it is a positive experience for you. Often you have eaten a spider before you knew what it was you were doing.

Sometimes you will receive the reward of gratitude from She Who Is Grateful for the Loss of a Spider, but you do not expect this gratitude for your action.

The cat will eat spiders as well, though you have a feeling that she takes pleasure in eating—or at least pleasure in toying with—the spiders. You would rather not eat them. But it is too late. And they taste wrong. Not like food, you think. Like spiders.

*Bees*

Bees are not so dangerous as wasps. If you manage to chew and swallow them before they notice, you will not even be stung. And bees, as you all know, are delicious.

*Moths*

Moths should always be spit back out when caught. They are not good to eat. And there is never enough of them to satisfy the urge to eat one. It is like eating air, and just about as tasty. So why bother?

## GRASS

You don't know why you eat the grass, but you do it, and it satisfies one of the requirements of your day. It takes you awhile to figure out what it is that has been nagging at you sometimes, but then you eat the grass, the long grass that grows near the fence or the grass that has begun to grow near the roses, and then you feel that the day has moved forward, that you can move on to the next thing, which might be a nap in the sandbox, or it might be half an hour standing at the back fence looking for the neighbor dog (this is a new neighbor, who claims to be mostly wolf, but who can't even see that there's a chase-worthy cat who lives in her yard), or it might be an hour of grooming your hindquarters (you've an itch back there that never really goes away for longer than a few moments).

## HUMAN WASTE

There are many kinds of human waste, much of it perfectly edible. You know that some judge you for eating this. Some will feel it is disgusting, and they would never eat such a thing. But you also know that those who would judge you for eating waste would also, when necessary, eat olives or fish. You will not eat olives or fish. You are principled and proud. There is a reason you and your ancestors have survived as a species for as long as you have. When you live in community with humans, you take what you can get, and you survive. Those who do not adapt to their environment, those who roam in packs and will eat only that which still has the heat of life in it, those species will perish. You and your kind will remain because you can survive on what has been discarded.

Your heritage is one of sustained adaptation and survival. There is no shame in that, and you will never pretend any shame. You are proud. So proud that you are unafraid to tip over the trash can in plain sight of He Who Removes the Best of the Trash to the Curb. He yells, "Hey, dammit, now I have to clean that up." You found what you smelled in there. You don't know what kind of food it was, but it was clearly food, and you take it behind the garage to eat it, just in case he recognizes that this was not waste but food, just in case he tries to take it from you and eat it himself.

(Only the baby has actually done this, taken the slice of cheese from you that you found on the floor, but you will never forget her taking it, because she was the one human in the universe that you couldn't growl and nip at for having taken the cheese. From then on, you wouldn't take any chances. It's always best to remove your discovery to a nearby safe location.)

## PREFERENCE

Though you hope nobody takes this the wrong way. Over all the other food you eat? Even steak? Even cheese? You really prefer hot dogs.

## 7

# REST AND SLEEP

Next to eating, sleeping is the most rewarding experience you know, and before you sleep you will always find the best place in which to sleep so that your sleep will be enhanced by your position in the universe. The best place to sleep is on your people's bed. You believe this is because your people have left something of themselves behind in the bed, and as you sleep your body is infused with this something.

## WHERE IS THE DOG?

Chances are very good that when someone says aloud, "Where is the dog?" you are actually asleep very near at hand, perhaps even beside the chair they are sitting in.

Even as you sleep you are aware of almost every move your people make. If one of them moves or changes position enough, you will wake up and look at them to see if they are about to offer you some of their attention. If not, you put your head back down and it is not long before you are back asleep.

## BEDDING DOWN

Before you lie down, you have to prepare your bed. This is done by circling your intended resting place. You cannot lie properly and relax until you've turned 'round on yourself approximately three and a half rotations. You may not turn more than four, or you will make yourself dizzy and have to pause, then start over at the beginning. You may not turn less than three, or you will not sleep peacefully, thinking perhaps there might have been a more restful position to sleep in had you turned just one half of a rotation more. When you have prepared your bed and dropped your body onto it, it is polite to release the air from your body in a long, nearly whistling sigh. This releases the tension not just from your body, but from the room you're sleeping in. Once you've done this, you may rest, and so may the world.

## FORCED AWAKE

Sleeping is an invitation to be forced awake. There are any number of ways in which you might be forced awake.

### By Your People

When you are asleep, you will most likely be disturbed (though *disturbed* isn't really the right word, because you are never actually disturbed when this happens so much as you are momentarily interrupted). You look at him tiredly, but you are glad he woke you. It means he would like to touch you or throw the ball or talk to you. He is paying attention to you and you do not miss the sleep. You will sleep again later. Soon you will very likely be asleep. Perhaps you have moved to be nearer to his chair because he woke you. You lie there now. He is about to say, "Where is the dog?" The sound of your collar moving when you lift your head tells him where you are. "There you are," he says. "Good dog."

## By the Kitten

If she comes toward you from the front, and acts as if she is about to pounce on your nose, you will growl at her. It is not a dangerous growl, and she seems to understand this, because she continues to approach, as if stalking you. Which is what she's doing. You recognize this playfulness as training behavior. She is training to be an adult cat. You will try to help her, as she is a member of your family now, but there is only so much you can do. Sometimes, all you can do is be the prey. You act as if you are a kind of dangerous prey, and when she approaches, you lift your paw and let it drop on her. She lets out a yawl, and this has been a good lesson.

If she approaches from behind, you flop your tail this way and that way, and she pounces on your tail. This is good agility training, you think. She will learn patterns and rhythm and how to attack. At the same time, you do not have much feeling in the end of your tail, so it doesn't hurt much when she gets her claws into you (and even if it did, you wouldn't let on to her that she had hurt you). You let her do this as long as she wants. She is still very young, and she will give up after awhile, off in search of a tissue or a sock.

## By the Noise

What was that? Did you hear that? Nobody heard it but you. You sound the alarm: "Rourourourou, rou, rou, rou, rourourourou, rou rou rou!"

Again! Did you hear that? Is it inside the house? Is it going to take your family away? Is it the lion? The UPS driver? "Rou rou rou." Apparently you have frightened them off, but you will keep barking just to make sure. You will keep barking until She Who Checks the Door checks the door and says, "There's nobody there, you silly dog." There are a few more barks left in you and you let them out. "Okay okay," she says, rubbing your head. "I get it. That's enough." You stop barking, and she kneels down and you lick her face. "Ack!" she says, pushing your face away.

You are so glad to be awake now. Look at all the joy filling up the room.

## By the Earth Moving

Once in awhile, the earth moves. It literally moves. All the earth. All over creation. You feel it and you hear the neighborhood dogs from one block to the next. First they go silent, then they report. The report does not sound good. What happens after the earth moves? The whole earth? Why does it do this? What will happen to you? What will happen to your family?

Luckily, you have a safe place when the earth moves.

Ever since they put in the bunk beds for the children, you have been able to crawl underneath them. When the earth moves, you crawl underneath. Later, your people will call for you. You do not move out of your place. You will not come out until you absolutely have to pee.

## Rest

You do not need rest. Rest is for weak dogs. You can chase the ball. You can chase the sled. You can chase the car. You can chase the cat. There is no reason for you to stop.

Except when you are tired.

It's probably time for a nap.

A nap is not actually rest. A nap is just a nap. It is sleep, and sleep is its own reward, like eating or chewing that place on your hindquarters that nags at you. You sleep. You are rewarded with sleep. Later, you will chase again. You will chase whatever it is that needs to be chased. And then you will sleep again.

This is how wonderful life can be. Every act can be this rewarding.

## MORE

There would be more to tell here, but every time you think about it, your head grows heavy and you have to find a good soft place to lie down.

# 8

# OUT OF DOORS

There is at least as much out of doors as there is indoors. As much to do and see. You sense that out of doors was the original home for dogs. But dogs have grown beyond that, recognizing that it is dog nature to adapt to humankind, to come inside and share their space and their warmth and their food. But it does not change the fact that when you are out of doors, you feel just as at home, if not more so, as when you are inside.

## S U N

Do you worship the sun? You do not. It is too much of a burden in the summertime and comes crashing down on you with the force of a fist. But in the early spring, those first few days when it is still cool outside and the sun is out, you sit in a patch of dirt and feel the cool earth on your belly while the heat massages your back. You keep your head up and wonder at the world, at the beauty of the world, at the surprise of finding such a world, and you watch for movement, though you will not chase squirrels or other dogs or joggers today. You will not bark or jump against the fence. You are in the glory of the sun and the earth. You are an essential piece of the sun and the earth. You have never been so alive and have never so well understood your position, your station, your calling. And when your people call to you, you leap to them. You have to tell them about this. Do they know this miracle? Have they been a part of this themselves? He takes you by your jowls and scratches and makes the noise that means he understands, and for this brief moment he is dog and you are people and they are the same. He does understand. It is why you adore him.

## RAIN

Sometimes water falls from the sky, and if it begins while you are out there, you sometimes believe you have caused the rain, and you try to trace your steps in bringing it on. If it rains for a very long time and your people have not responded to your scratching and jumping at the back door, you forget about what you did to cause it, and you simply lie in one of the places that is protected from the rain falling on you. Though the rain shows no sign of stopping, it has always done so in the past, so you believe it will probably stop again this time.

If it is raining before you go outside, you will hesitate at the back door. "Oh, don't be such a wimp," says He Who Opens the Door. "Go on." He gives you a little push, and out you go. If you hurry, you can get back to the door in time for him to notice you there, to let you inside and rub you with a towel. Thank goodness for the towel. It contains a kind of warmth found in no other portable item in the house. The towel must contain some kind of magic. You wish that you had a towel of your very own.

## SNOW

When it is snowing, you do not have time to consider it, to think about it. You have time only to be in it, to catch the snowballs that the children are throwing at you, to chase the world at top speed, to gallop through it and jump into the air and run and run and be fully aware of just exactly how marvelous this world is.

## WIND

The air blowing around you cuts into your body. You bite at the wind, hoping to make it stop, but it does not stop. You seek shelter from the wind. The wind changes many of your regular activities. You will not spend time at the back gate while the wind is blowing. You take your shelter near the back door, hoping they will come to the back door soon to let you inside.

## CHAIN

There is a chain in the backyard that they attached to your collar once or twice. One time they tied you to a different chain, which you snapped within the first ten minutes of being tied out. When tied out on this new chain, you first pulled on the chain until you were able to work your collar off, and when they put it back on you, tighter this time, you wrapped the chain around the children's swing set so you had no room for movement and ended up spending two hours on a one-foot lead, just next to the slide, sleeping in the shade of the slide and waiting for them to come home. You think they have given up on using the chain, but it still hangs there on the post as if in warning. Warning of what, you aren't quite sure.

## DOGHOUSE

There is a small house outside that is supposed to be for you, but it does not remind you of your crate, and it does not remind you of a home. You have been inside this house only three times. There is always a better place to find shelter during a rainstorm. The children have taken over the house. It has become theirs, especially good for pretending to be a dog.

## THUNDER

When the world explodes in thunder, you hope not to be outside. You hope to be inside where you can hide under the bunk beds. If you are outside, you will leap at the back

door, hoping to be let in. If no one
answers, you will leap the fence
into the neighbor's backyard.
Her gate is easier to open, so
you open it and run to the
front door. You leap at the
front door, hoping to be let in. If you are not let in, you
will take refuge here on the front porch, as close to the
house as possible, as far from the sound of thunder as possible.

You watch for Dog Who Escapes during thunder-
storms. If he passes, you will encourage him to take shelter with you. But he will not. He will simply pass, hoping
to outrun the thunder.

## TREE

Trees have many different uses for all kinds of animals.
Some, such as cats or squirrels, use trees for escape when
you chase them. This is why you prefer to have few trees
in your yard. No use helping them escape, you think.

### Young Tree

There used to be a tree there, in the yard. A small tree. You
remember it. But you were very young. You chewed it
until there was nothing left of it, and when your people
discovered what had happened, they put you inside the
house. Later they dug up the tree and removed it from the
yard. And thank goodness. It was just in the wrong place.

## Old Tree

Though animals that can climb often escape into them, old trees can be useful, especially in the summer, when the full force of the sun is trying to topple you. You lie in the shade of the tree and wait for the shade to pass by. Every so often you will move to the coolest part of the shade. Every so often the leaves will rustle in the breeze, reminding you that summer does not last forever.

## Branch

A tree branch is no longer a tree branch when it has fallen to the ground. It is a stick, and a stick is a well-known dog toy. You may chase it or chew it or bury it. It is a toy regardless, and if you know which tree it came from, you will thank the tree for its sacrifice. You will stop near the tree and sniff the tree, looking for the scent of another dog, and you will surely find it, for anywhere you go, another dog has already been there. You leave your scent there as well so you will be able to locate yourself in the continuity of dogs.

# BACK DOOR

When you want to go inside, you stand at the back screen door and you look inside. If they don't notice you there, you leap against the door. You've developed a facility with your leap, and you can land on the steps without falling, without rolling down to the bottom of the steps like you used to. You will leap three times consecutively, then you will look through the glass, waiting. You will wait the amount of time it takes sound to travel into the house and up the stairs and into the bedroom (obviously they are asleep in bed or they would let you in immediately), then you leap three more times consecutively and wait again (the same amount of time, which you know is an approximation, but you think you have it worked out pretty closely).

## ESCAPEE

You know what is going to happen when you escape from the yard. You know where you are going to go, and you will be looking primarily for the neighborhood smells, the neighborhood dogs and their smells, and you will find them and you will smell them, and you will visit those you know and those you don't know, and you will come to places that are familiar and unfamiliar, and you will linger on certain smells to be certain that they are familiar, that they are memorized, and you will draw a picture from each of these smells, and the picture creates a landscape.

You know that if you wander long enough, it will come down to this: someone will come who is friendly and has a nice tone to his voice, and you will follow him and he will put you in the back of his truck and you will go for a ride. His truck smells of every dog in the universe. This truck is outside the universe and inside it at the same time. It is like a spacecraft, taking you out of the world, and it will insert you into a kind of time machine where every moment is a million years, and though the truck takes you to a place you hate, locked into a cement and steel cell, you also love it because it is a cacophonous, riotous place from which you know you will eventually be plucked by your people. They have come to retrieve you before, and they will come again. You mostly lie still and wait for them. And people come and talk to you. And people come and walk you in the grassy place outside the building, but even outside the building there are so many smells, so much noise, that you cannot locate yourself in the world.

When will they come for you? It has been years, hasn't it? People come and look at you. People come. But none are your people. They will come soon. They have to come soon.

## 9

# OF WORK AND OF PLAY

### Y O U R  B A R K

You didn't know right away that you could do that. But, just a few moments after discovering that your territory can be expanded by throwing your voice, you break into a chorus of "rou rou rou rou rou" that would make your mother proud. Why did it take you so long to discover this talent? Perhaps if there had been another dog in your home, you would have discovered it earlier.

And there is He Who Stays at Home All Day, announcing: "Knock it off!" You try to make this noise he has just made, but it only continues "rou rou rou rou." Perhaps it is he that is doing it wrong: "Quiet!" he says. "When did you become a barking dog?"

"Rou rou rou rou."

"Get in here."

"Rou rou rou rou."

"Come on. Get in here. Now."

He has such variety in tone and volume and pattern. His voice is out of control. You had not really noticed this before either. But now that you notice it, you wonder if it doesn't embarrass him to be unable to make such a beautiful noise as you do. You lower your head as you enter, hoping to make yourself smaller, to make yourself less proud of your accomplishment.

"That's right," he says. "Get in there. No barking. No more barking."

You will become an artist. You will perfect the sound of your own voice. Yours will be like no other.


## S H O P P I N G

This is paradise. When He Who Drives holds the car door open and says "Come on," which is meant to indicate that you are to come along for the ride, you think you are going on an adventure to a new open space, a new park or playground, a new river or wilderness. Instead he brings you to a kind of amusement park, full of toys and treats and friendly faces, humans and dogs and cats and caged birds and innumerable odors, food odors and animal odors and creaturelike odors that you cannot describe or understand. The world inside is overwhelming. Luckily he has put the harness on you so you are not tempted to run free through the aisles.

Correction. You are tempted, but the harness keeps you in position, keeps you near him on the lead, trying to focus on any one item in the place. It is impossible.

What is this place?

He appears to be making some kind of selection. He takes items from shelves, then holds a rawhide bone up to your nose and says, "You want one of these?"

Whatever he has said, the answer must be yes. You sense that no matter what you would actually answer, he wants you to answer yes.

He takes several items toward the front of the store, where there is some kind of exchange, of words and papers and rawhide. You return with him to the car and sit in the passenger seat. He gives you the rawhide bone, but you don't begin to chew it right away. First you have to let him know somehow that he has to bring you back here some day. You circle in the chair as well as you can, then lick the side of his face. "Okay okay," he says, "settle down now." You turn once more and sit on the chair. You would lie on the chair but it isn't big enough for you. Forget it. You cannot even think of the rawhide bone right now. You'll wait until you get home. Right now you have a lot to think about. That place was fabulous. Terrifyingly fabulous.

## HERDING THE CHILDREN

When the children are playing in the yard, you make sure they do not run into the street. You circle them and you run from here to there and from there to here. You are always busy at work when the children are in the yard. Even in the backyard, you must pay attention. You never know when one of them is going to bolt. They are unpredictable. They might make a run for it. You cannot tell what they are about to do as you can with the adults. They are very busy and seemingly random in their activities. You are very busy making sure they are safe and healthy. This is important. These are your children.

When they are playing safely on the swings or drawing on the cement with chalk, you lie in the dirt near the garden gate and watch them closely, head down between your paws so that they will forget they are being watched. If they forget they are being watched, they will be less likely to make a run for it. In this way they are very much like puppies.

## C R O W S

The crows sometimes circle near your house, and this makes you anxious. If the crows are close enough for you to have some effect on them, you will "rou rou rou" at them. But most of the time you seem to have no effect on the crows. Sometimes they come for a discarded piece of food, an activity you understand. But their approach is disquieting. Sometimes, too, they will attack a dying animal, and this also seems entirely natural. But they seem so aggressively apart from the rest of the world, as if their food was never anything but food.

This wildness has been driven from you, it seems. You are drawn to it, but you recognize it as other than yourself. You do not take a moral stance because the activity is amoral. You observe and you learn. This is the way of the crows. You hope to never be seen as weak in their eyes. Surely, given the opportunity to do so, they would come for you—circle you. So you assert yourself to them when they are nearby. Whether they respond or not is beside the point. You know they can hear you.

## RUNNER

When the runner passes, you raise your hackles and make yourself known. You announce your property and warn him away. He is running from you. He is running first toward you, then away. You chase him a bit across the front yard, and before you know what has happened, you've jumped the fence. You didn't mean to jump the fence, and actually you'd forgotten that you could jump the fence (only performing this feat of acrobatics when thunder or fireworks forces you into adrenaline-charged madness). You sort of jump the fence and sort of climb it, using your back feet to gain purchase on the cyclone fence, and you are up and over. The runner turns and kicks at your face. You have no choice. You bite at his leg. Not at his leg, really, but at the material that flaps just loose of his actual leg. You pull at the cloth that covers his leg and he trips. He falls and gets up and kicks at you again, but He Who Puts You in the Backyard during the day has come out of the house and is calling for you, probably praising you and telling you how wonderfully you've protected them, but before you know what has happened, he has tackled you.

Your brain does not work fast enough to know what

has happened, really, but you know that you have also bitten He Who Feeds You Scraps of Meat. This does not seem like the right thing to have done, but he has both arms around you and is holding you to the ground with all of his weight, and you struggle against his weight, but there is little you can do. Your confusion is compounded by a pain in your rib cage. A pain that screams. It screams to be released, and you've bitten him again, though this time a bit softer, finally realizing that biting him is not such a good idea, and you sense already that this will not be a good day.

All that you know to do now is run to the house, run inside the door and wait, bark and scream in a pain still wanting to be released. You bark and wait for what will come.

What will come?

You go to the sofa and lie against the pain and whimper, wondering if you will be eaten by crows.

## BALL

You will chase almost any ball that is in motion not because it is a ball, but because it is in motion. Motion is irresistible to you. You must chase it.

### Tennis Ball

You will chase the tennis ball because it is moving, because it is in motion. He Who Says "Drop It" will throw the tennis ball, and you will chase after it. You will bring it back toward him and come near, but you will not drop the tennis ball. Dropping the tennis ball would mean that he would have it again, but you have it, and it is his job to get it away from you. This is the game. Him trying to win the ball from you. When he reaches toward you, you bound away. If he has a treat, a piece of cheese or kibble, you cannot resist and you will drop the ball in exchange for the treat, but you will try to pick up the ball again once the treat is in your mouth. Sometimes you are successful at this. When you are successful at this, he will throw up his hands and walk toward the door, exasperated by something. It must be too cold for him. You wish he would stay out and play this game with you. You drop the ball by the back steps and follow him up to the door. He is ignoring you now. It must be the cold. He'll get his gloves and come back out. You love the gloves because they are leather and you secretly want to chew them. You know he'll be back with the gloves and maybe the stocking cap. He'll be back any minute.

### Ball in the River

Now he's done it. He's thrown it into the river. You've done this before. You've retrieved it for him before, and you imagine you should protect him from losing the ball in the river by hiding it somewhere that he won't be able to find it, but secretly you enjoy it a bit, so you jump into the river and retrieve the ball and you bring it to him. What has the ball done to him? He throws it into the river again. We've come all the way out here just to throw the ball into the

river. The ball begins to move downstream almost immediately, and the current is strong. It's stronger than you were
expecting. You leap into the water, and you weren't expecting it to be quite this cold, but you suppose it shouldn't surprise you. It has been cold for several days. Maybe weeks.
Maybe a few years it has been cold. You aren't sure. But
right now, in the water, yes, it's been cold forever. And anyway, you're used to it in a matter of moments. That's the
secret. Jumping in all at once. Everyone knows that.

But the ball. The ball is floating away. Is it getting farther from you? Maybe not. Or is that the ball? Was it a ball
or a stick? Or a piece of bark? Or a wave? Or . . . no,
there's the ball. There it is. It's just a bit away from you
still. There it is. Just off over there. Somewhere. Wasn't it?
Just over there. Yes. Over there.

You see it now. It's in sight. The river is calmer here.
You have a bit of a swim to get there, but you'll get there.
You'll get there. You'll get there. There it is. You'll get
there. You've got it. You've got it now. You've got it!

You turn around to swim back to shore, and you're
swimming for the shore, and you see the shore, but you
don't see He Who Is Angry at the Ball. He is out of sight.
And all you hear is the rushing water. You must have
floated downstream a bit. You try to swim upstream, but
the current is too strong. And all you hear is current. All
you hear is river. Why was he so angry at the ball that he
threw it into the river? Why?

Finally, you exit the river, and still the sound of the river
is strong, but you also hear the sound of his voice. He's call-

ing you from upstream, and now you have the difficult journey back. You have to make your way through the bramble and brush to where he stands on the riverbank. Could he not have followed you down the riverbank as you went? Could he not have made his way through bramble and brush? Perhaps not. Perhaps he is too human for that. You know he is too human for that. He is so very little dog.

And there he is. And he seems happy to see you. Genuine happiness. He bares his teeth, and you have known him long enough to know this is a sign of happiness rather than aggression. He leans down to you and rubs your head. You are satisfied with this, and you shake one more time for him. He backs away as you shake, and he laughs a deep and forthright laugh that must release a great deal of gas from his body. This must feel extremely good because he continues to smile. You know you should protect him from the ball now, but you don't. You drop the ball at his feet, and as it turns out he's as angry at this ball as he is happy to see you. He picks up the ball immediately and throws it back into the river.

You will get it back one more time. Perhaps this time you will hide it from him. You are worried he is going to burst a vein. But then again this is so very fun, you can't imagine actually hiding the ball, and you decide you won't. You are an optimist. He'll be okay.

### Snowball

When it snows and the snow is on the ground, He Who Throws the Ball of Snow is able to produce a seemingly endless supply of very fragile balls from the snow itself. You stand some distance away and he throws the ball, sometimes very high in the air or sometimes directly at you, and you attempt to catch the ball in your mouth and it explodes there in a kind of frigid tempest of water. The snow covering this ball is cold and wet and melts in your mouth. The ball itself has disappeared. Utterly vanished. He produces another one, though. Where do they all come from?

## F R I S B E E

The Frisbee game is much like the ball game, except the Frisbee somehow travels much farther, much slower, and manages to float in the air until you are able to catch up to it, to leap into the air and snatch it, almost as if you're snatching a flying animal (such as a bird) from the air.

After you catch it and return it, He Who Flings the Frisbee appears to want the Frisbee back. There is a complex set of rules he has to obey before you will give it to him. You never remember what the rules are until he's taken the Frisbee away from you. Then you remember. The rules are that he has to get the Frisbee away from you somehow and you have to keep from giving it to him.

If he is unable to take the Frisbee from you, you will chew it to pieces.

## SQUEAKY HAND TOY

You sometimes feel ridiculous doing it, but when she puts on the squeaky hand toy, you bite and claw and chew at it. She is usually sitting, watching the pictures move on the box in the living room, and she is squeaking the squeaker in the squeaky hand toy, and you are going mad with the desire to make the squeaky hand toy a servant to your needs, your needs to pounce and chew and love the toy. It must obey you.

Yes, you know that the squeaky hand toy is nothing more than a cover on her hand, and is nothing more than her hand making the squeaky hand toy squeak, but you are full of joy and need when she squeaks it nonetheless. Adoration! Joy! More, more, more!

## LEAD

One of your jobs when you walk on a lead is to pull along He Who Will Walk You on a Lead. He is slow and if you don't pull, you will never get anywhere, never do anything, never discover what is new in the world. It is hard enough as it is, living in a place where you are fenced in most of the day. It is difficult to find the news. It is difficult to transmit information. You have to speak loudly to be heard. Very little other sensory information passes from you to the community because you are so fenced in. So you must cover as much ground as possible during your walk. You must pull him. You must make sure that he walks at a sufficient speed.

He will make you turn at this corner. You know he will make you stop and turn. He will not continue toward the house with the two messenger dogs with sharp barks that sound like "rawr, rawr, rawr, rawr . . . rawr, rawr, rawr, rawr," always in staccato series of four, endlessly. You want to go there and listen to them, to find out who has passed recently, who has come in to the neighborhood, who is free and who is loved. But he makes you turn.

You can already smell them. And they smell you. And they begin to bark.

"Rawr, rawr, rawr, rawr . . . rawr, rawr, rawr, rawr."

You cannot even properly answer. You are wearing the face harness. You do not even try to answer, knowing that your voice is altered and miniature while wearing the face harness. But you are also glad of the face harness. It would be much more difficult to pull him without it. Your lead pulls too much on your neck, and that hurts. When you're in the face harness, you can properly pull him, and so you pull him.

Come on come on come on come on. You have a lot of space to cover and not much time to cover it in.

## STAY

You have been asked to "stay." You have been first asked to "sit," and then asked to "stay." You know several things about this. When your people return from inside the building, they will pour affection on you, and they will come bearing a snack of some kind. Usually the snack will be some kind of bread or pastry. As you are sitting near the entrance to the building, people will pass and talk to you. You will use your friendly, approachable face, but you will remain sitting because you know it is expected of you, and if you don't do it properly, you risk losing the treat, although you also know that you don't really risk losing the treat because your people are incapable of leaving a building without bringing you a treat. But you will lose something. Although that isn't right, because loss is a bit of a foreign concept to you. You understand that there might be the possibility of "loss," but it doesn't make sense to you because now there is this reality, here and now, of people passing and praising you, and in a few moments or minutes or years your people will exit the building and praise you and give you a treat. What keeps you seated, then, is something else. It is the possibility of the voice your people use when you do stand to greet the strangers. When they come out of the building and you are not sitting and staying, they speak to you with the voice that buckles your legs, that pushes down on your entire body and causes you to shake. What on earth do they put in their voice that makes you do this?

There they are. Do you see them? Do they see you? Should you stand? Can you stand now? Can you greet them and love them and lick them? No. Not yet. Wait. Wait. Wait. Now!

## O F F

When they come into the house, they want you to "sit." You know they want you to sit. But they are so high. So very high. How can you sit? How can you stay sitting? Don't they know if you sit too long, your blood will stop? Don't they know how dangerous it is, when you are this happy, when you are this close to them, when you are activating every light in your body, don't they know that sitting will only shut you down? Very dangerous. You have to get up. You have to jump a little and beg for attention. You have to jump up and find their face. Then beg for forgiveness. Then sit. Sit and wait for them. Always you are waiting for them.

## P A R K

This is the park. Sometimes, if the park is relatively empty of people and other dogs, you will be allowed off the lead. If you are allowed off the lead, you are expected to stay close to your people and not chase after whatever it is you might be inclined to chase after. There are many things you are inclined to chase after, but you know that if you chase after them, you will soon be back on the lead, because it causes displeasure for your people when you leave their side and chase or otherwise disappear. You do not like to cause them any kind of displeasure. Ever. You will try. You are filled with the kind of joy only to be found in the park off your lead, unfettered and with your people and ready to run and return, run and return.

But what was that? A squirrel?

There are some things so attractive and elusive that you simply cannot resist.

## PICKUP

You ride in the back. You stand forward in the bed of the pickup, your head over the edge, the wind flapping your ears, the sound of it like the sound of wind. When traveling especially fast, it becomes difficult to breathe, but you continue to breathe, and you continue to keep yourself here, even when he turns, even when it seems you will lose your footing and be slung from the rig. You are not. This is exhilarating, this speed. You cannot approach this speed on your own. This is the only way. Why would anybody ever travel any other way?

But when you stop, when you leap from the bed of the pickup, you remember, when you run, all four legs in sync with one another, never seeming to touch the ground except for a millimoment, you can fly. Perhaps you do not travel as fast as you would in the pickup, but by yourself, all on your own, under your own power, you fly.

## VOICE

"Go for a walk?" she says, and she uses the tone of voice that means you are about to go for a walk. Sometimes you are able to communicate perfectly with your people, and this is one of those times. You like to go for a walk with She Who Releases You because she will release you from the lead at some point, at which time you may chase squirrels. Or she will bring the ball and throw it and you will chase that. Then she comes toward you, surprising you with a second ball, and you will drop the first to pick up the second, and when you drop the first to pick up the second, she will pick up the first and throw that one, and the two of you will traverse whatever territory she's chosen for this game. Though this game seems to have no rules, it is also perfectly defined, and it is not so much that there are no rules as the rules are agonizingly simple, to the point of indescribability. The two of you communicate in neither your language nor hers. You simply exchange knowledge of the game. You suspect some shared kinship. But it isn't worth overexamining. Fetch, exchange, fetch, exchange. The simplicity is one of the most beautiful things you know of. You would follow her anywhere.

## DIFFERENCE

You suppose there is some dividing line between work and play, and if you considered it, you would be able to define each activity you performed as either work or play. But so far, in this life, as this dog, with these people, you have found no use for such a line. They are the same thing, and you will not examine your activities beyond the knowledge that all activities you pursue with your people are both work and play, and they make you full up with life.

## 10

# GNOSIS

Y ou do not ask many questions of your life. You simply are.

---

### DOGNESS

*Dogness* is a word that does not translate well into the language of your people. Some people, you have noticed,
seem to have some access to a kind of Peopleness, though
you are sure that peopleness is different from dogness in
some essential (or nonessential) way. Those who are connected to their peopleness are able to communicate with
you better than other people do. They still use words, but
somehow connect their peopleness to your dogness, and
you are able to understand them.

Some call their peopleness Spirit. Some call it Essence.
Others call it Chi. Whatever it is, it is the thing you use
to communicate with those who can sense it. You wonder why people are so disconnected from it. You think it
might have something to do with the television.

## S I M P L E   D E S I R E

Sometimes, every once in awhile (at least once a day) when you stand by the door and then approach one of your people and then return to the door and they open the door and you stand at the door and look outside but don't go outside, they will say, "What? What do you want?" You simply gaze at them. Honestly, you aren't quite sure, and you were hoping they would know.

## F A I T H

You have no need of faith. Faith implies that there is some question. There is no question. There just is.

## C R E A T I O N

You do not often stop to think who created all of this. Who created you. Who created them. Who created the black rubber bouncing thing. You do not often stop to think about what comes after (which is a part of "creation" as much as death is a part of birth, and this should be obvious but you have a feeling that for some, these things need to be spelled out). You do not often think about what comes later than the time that is now. And it is not because you are not a complex enough being to do so. You do not often stop to think of these things because the answers are obvious. The answers are so obvious that there are no words for the answers.

## B A P T I S M

There are friends of yours that participate in their baths as if it were a good thing, a positive moment in their lives, as if this act will improve who they are as a Being in This World. Though you do not hold this as true for yourself, you understand this need on their part, this desire, to allow the bath to occur and to pretend that it is a kind of cleansing. They have been indoctrinated by their people, and they do as expected of them. You believe they are foolish to believe in such things. But then again, they believe you are foolish to allow the mailman as much access to the house as he receives. You have made your peace with the mailman. His packages are generally small and unobtrusive.

He Who Delivers Unknowable Packages . . . he is another story.

## C O M M U N I O N

You do not eat except when they eat. Sometimes they eat first, and then they feed you. When they feed you first, you wait, because something inside you tells you to wait, that if they decide to share the food in your bowl with you, you must share it with them. He Who Usually Feeds

You in the Evening will tell you to go ahead and eat, but you do this only with reluctance. She Who Fills the Bowl and also Fills the Water will feed you and let the food sit and you will wait until they are also eating, also nearby where you can see and hear them eating. Then you will eat. You will share food with your people in this way. And sometimes they will drop crusts for you. Dropped crusts are to be eaten immediately, or they might be taken away.

You trust that, though you now eat last, some day you will eat first.

When given a beef bone, you save some of it. Somehow you know that you are not supposed to save any of it, that you are supposed to eat it all and it will be exactly enough for you to eat, but you save some of it anyway, and you will either bury it or leave it somewhere in the yard where you may remember it, or you will leave it near the back step where it can be seen that you are saving some of the beef bone, so that they will know that you can conserve as well as devour. This beef bone leaves you conflicted. You should eat it. But something makes you leave some there. For next time. For tomorrow.

Having relied on people for so long has modified your species in larger ways than you imagine, so that you do some of the broken things they do, not out of habit but because it has become your nature to do so. You like your people, though, and are not concerned that acting in small ways as they do will cause you any harm. In the long run, you will all end up in the same place, at the same time, with the same set of buried bones.

## R E W A R D

You do not believe in rewards. Or rather, you do not understand them. You do not believe that the kibble He Who Said Sit offers you is a reward so much as it is a small bit of food. If it pleases him and he will feed you when you perform some act, then you will repeat this performance. You live to give all of yourself in the service of companionship, in the service of equality and compatibility, of being with your people, of running, alongside or behind or in front, but always with, as if space means nothing.

You live in service to human nature, that fickle, unrewarding beast, and if the reward were pulled away, or replaced by something else, you would not miss it—you do not need it and do not recognize it. You simply run.

## M O T I V A T I O N

What motivates you?

Food.

What makes you move from one place to another (such as moving away from the gate where you have been barking for almost an hour to the back door where He Who Would Like You to Come is standing)?

Food. The prospect or the reality of food. Or the sense that there is food nearby. Or that there has been food and someone has hidden the food somewhere. The food is in the food box and someone needs to come and scoop it out into your bowl. Is there food? Have they fed you yet?

Though you are motivated by food, you will generally not put yourself in danger because of it. The opposing danger, the danger of starvation, would have to be immediate and great. And for some reason, you are always certain that there will be food. Even when your people have forgotten to feed you directly, there has been food from somewhere. From the trash, sometimes, or from the plum tree, or from the man who walks past eating bagels who sometimes tosses you a taste. This seems natural. The world will feed you.

## ARRIVAL AND LOSS

Is this one staying? Is she staying? Will she be here tomorrow? And tomorrow's tomorrow? And the tomorrow of tomorrow's tomorrow?

How about yesterday? Why wasn't she here yesterday?

Is she staying? Is that an answer? What are they saying?

Will she be here a few minutes from now? A few moments? Will you be able to play together in the daytime, in the morning time, in the nighttime? Will you sleep in the same room, on the same bed, on the same sofa? Will her rules be your rules? Can you bite her ears?

You will bite her ears.

Is she staying?

Never mind. You don't understand what they're saying to you, but it seems to mean that this one is staying, at least until tomorrow. You'll act as if she is staying and mourn her leaving once she's gone.

## LITTER

When they come home, they are without the new baby. You knew the new baby was supposed to be coming home with them, but they are without the new baby. They still have the old baby, of course (whom you have begun to call She Who Often Stumbles So Stand Out of Her Path). At times like these you wish you could communicate better with them, for you understand these things as no one else understands them.

You could help them. You know you could.

You were born, of course, of a litter. Your litter was six. There was one, the one you knew as Third, who did not survive. You knew her as Third because she was third of the litter. She came after First and Second, and before you, who was Fourth, and also before Fifth and Sixth. These are not names that you held for long, of course, but you remember them especially because Third remained Third. She was born without ever moving, without ever breathing, without ever nuzzling or nursing or biting the loose skin at the back of your neck.

You did not know much about Third because no one ever talked about her. But you sensed her. There you were, nursing, suckling, and you felt her absence, and also her presence, there at the nipple next to yours, nuzzling and sucking and not nuzzling and not sucking. Perhaps it was a feeling passed to you from your mother, perhaps a feeling passed in the milk. It was an ache for the absence there. But you found yourself moving to that nipple. Taking the milk from there instead, and moving back and forth, alternating between feedings, from one nipple to another, from Third's milk to yours. None of your other littermates even seemed to choose a specific nipple of their own, but they also never used yours or Third's. And you found your mother favoring you, licking you first, licking you again after the rest were licked, finding a warm place for you in the curl of her body in the coldest part of the night, moving you sometimes so that you would be against her.

When they picked you out of the box, your people had thought you were the runt, the small one, the one who would always be smaller, would always need special care. But you grew faster than the others, and you felt special, as if you were needed in the world, as if you had some purpose other than chasing squirrels or leading or following or chasing away predators. You do not feel the need to lead a pack. You are a modern dog, and more connected to your dogness and also to peopleness. The modern dog does not necessarily think in terms of "pack," since this is a social construct. It is not a biological necessity but one established to stabilize an otherwise unstable group of animals. You do not feel the need to satisfy a societal order, Alpha, Beta, Etcetera. Indeed, when within a group of peers, your denial of the pack order makes you most likely nominated Alpha, and the more you deny your superiority, the more it is offered. So you avoid peers, mostly. You keep to yourself and spend more time with your people (who have just arrived home without the new baby).

You wonder if they remember your own litter, your children, your puppies, numbers one through four. The four who also became three. The one who did not survive from your litter was also third, and so you have always thought of her as Three, so she seems to have a stronger kinship with your sibling. Sometimes you think that your daughter's death was a product of your future loneliness, of having to lose all of your litter to strangers. Or rather your daughter, Three, was attempting to prepare you for this loneliness by leaving early, by disappearing into her siblings, her spirit into theirs, as if there really is only one spirit and they all share it, dipping into the same pool for their first sip of life.

There are times when you wonder if there weren't others in that litter that simply didn't show themselves—they knew too much of this world already, perhaps, and therefore refused to be born. Perhaps there are still two clinging to your womb. They are buried in your heart. You feel them every day, pulling you to the ground at times, pulling you up again, pulling you forward or backward. You watch your people now as they come home without the new baby, without their Three, as they sit in the great room and hold their grief within themselves, their arms wrapped arm over chest, arm over chest, speaking but not listening. You wish you could communicate with them somehow.

"That pain," you would tell them, "that pain is important." You try to tell them this by coming near and looking into their eyes. "That pain will become the thing you treasure most," you want to say. "It is really a kind of joy, when you feel it long enough, when you allow yourself to have it long enough, when you allow it to take you over and transform your heart, to massage and beat and become your heart." Perhaps they understand some small part of this, because they do rub your ears and touch your head. They do take your head in their hands and talk to you. Perhaps they are saying, "I know, I know. But I cannot be where you are right now. I can't be there." You know this. You are a part of this. There is nothing about this you do not understand.

"She came here this morning," you would tell them. "She has been here all along. She will stay here. With you. With us. Seek her out, but don't worry. Even if you don't find her, she will find you."

You sit there beside them and hope they will notice the deep understanding in your eyes. Moments pass. Days. A week and a month and a year. A hand reaches toward you and rests on your head, and a scratch behind the ear. Sometimes the only way for you to communicate with them is through time. Simple day after day.

## STRUGGLE

You see your people struggle with hardship and anxiety and work and relationships. You will help each of them in a different, individual fashion.

### She Who Carries the Weight of the World

You know she does not mean to or want to, but whatever the difficulty, she carries it on her shoulders, setting the weight of the world's troubles against the strength of her back. Though sometimes you believe her to be the strongest of your people, you also believe she can be the most vulnerable to pain, to anxiety, to sorrow. She tries not to show it, and to the rest of the world, to her friends and the other people in her life, it may seem that she is just fine, that her world is as it should be. But you see something else. The slightest difference in her expression, in the way she holds her shoulders, in the way she gestures for you to come closer. There is a catch in her motion. It's the sort of thing that could keep her from moving forward, like a command to "sit . . . stay," that while she may not understand what the command actually means, it keeps her from standing and moving forward.

When she sits on the sofa, and when she is otherwise unencumbered (by cat or child or husband), you sit as near to her as you can, watching her closely. Sometimes all you can do is let someone know that you are there if they need you. Even if they never need you, you are there.

### He Who Sits on His Head

When he is not with one of his friends, leaping from the furniture, riding his bicycle, hitting a ball into the neighbor's yard (a ball you will try to catch in the air), he is sometimes upstairs watching the television. The strange colors on the television sometimes resemble actual items in the house. Sometimes even a cat or dog. Actually, quite often a dog, one who tries to talk to people, one who proclaims "Rooby Rooby Roo!" This is nothing like an actual dog, but there must be something intriguing to him about this dog, so you watch it with him, hoping to learn something. While he watches the television, he often sits on his head, his legs tossed over the back of the sofa, his feet against the wall. If he would sit still, you would try to sit next to him, hoping to see what he sees.

Instead you lie on the floor and watch the television. It makes no sense at all, but that's okay. You have a feeling it isn't supposed to make any sense. It has some other purpose. Or no purpose at all. Like chasing the cat. No purpose but the act itself.

## She Who Was Once the Baby

You do not call her The Baby very often anymore. She has become louder recently, as if being stepped on many times a day. You respect this because she is in competition for attention with her sibling. Or rather, she believes she is in competition, and must scream and stomp to get the attention of her parents, which reminds you of puppies, who will likely jump at your mouth and ears and nose to get your attention, will pierce your skin with their needlelike teeth when they could simply come and lie near their mother, touch their mother with their noses, and lie down and look up at her with eyes that do not compare in loveliness to anything else on earth. Puppies who did this would receive attention first. It is a simple act of faith for a puppy to learn this, and you try to teach this to She Who Was Once the Baby by your example, by giving her attention when she is the most still, coming to her and giving her attention and grooming and licking her.

She seems to treat this as an opportunity to scream, which makes you believe she's not getting it yet. She'll get it eventually. You don't know how long it takes to train a human child, but apparently it can take a very long time.

### He Who Does Not Understand the Walk

When he is very stressed or disturbed or out of sorts, he takes you for a walk. You do not walk with him as much as you do with her. When you pull on the lead, he stops walking altogether. You don't understand how this works, how to get him to go faster. You know it will relieve some of the stress of his life if you can get him to walk faster, to act as if he was a dog, to simply run whatever is bothering him right out of his body. You would think that the harder you pulled, the faster he would walk. But this isn't so. He slows or stops and says, "Whoah. Get in." When he does this, he will not continue until you back up and sit near him. As soon as you sit, he will move forward. This does not make any sense to you. Is he taunting you? Is he going to take his aggression out on you?

No he isn't. You almost wish that he would, so he wouldn't have that look on his face so often. You wish there was more you could do.

"Okay, let's go," he says. And you're off again. Too slow again. But better slow than not at all.

## HIGHER BEING

Of course you believe in a higher being. What kind of question is that? Of course. For instance: the voice on the telephone, who is the same person as the voice on the television with the moving pictures, who is the same person as the voice of the higher being that you sometimes hear just before falling asleep, when you lift up your head and go to the window and look out, looking for him or her, for the voice, to say hello, to make sure they know where to find you.

## GRACE

No one has ever described grace to you, and no one needs to. You are the living definition of grace.

When they are gone for a very long time, for days and weeks and months, you love them.

When they have left you outside in the rain or the sleet or the hot, hot sun, you love them.

When they yell at you to get down from the sofa or not to drink from the water dispenser or not to chew the Superman action figure, though you are not quite sure what it is that you have done that is wrong, you love them.

You respond to their touch with love.

You respond to their ire with love.

You respond to their love with love.
You respond with love.
You are grace.

## S H A L O M

You do not simply greet as others greet. You are not interested in what has happened between the time you last saw
your people and their return home. You are not interested
in scolding them. You do not want to hold them account-
able for having been away for so long. You simply want
them to know how utterly overjoyed you are that they are
alive, that they are in your presence. And it is not a face
that you wear. It is a truth that you hold. You are filled
with the most joyous kind of joy when they appear, a kind
of peaceful joy, an everlasting peace that begins with this
moment and goes on forever.

When the car arrives in the driveway after being gone
for fifteen minutes to the grocery store, when the taxi door
opens and you hear the sound of her shoes on the sidewalk
and her voice saying something incomprehensible to the
driver, when you wake in the morning and remember
where you are, whose bed you have slept at the foot of, and
how easy it is to wake them with a lick in the face, the sun
still early on the horizon, the day still partly night, you find
your shalom in this moment, and though you cannot put
it into human words, you hope to share it with your
expression, with the face and body of joy that you are not
sure a human person can understand except as children. It

is a joy that people seem to block from returning to you, even at their most joyous. It is a joy that you wish you could spill into their hearts because it feels so much like the thing they are truly missing. Truly missing. It is a joy that says "Yes!" It is a joy that says "I'll love you forever!" And the only way you can truly feel it is when you share it. And you share it. Yes. You'll love them forever.

## COMPLICATION

You know that your people are prone to overcomplication, so you would like to simplify your message here one last time, and then that will be all. You will leave them to their lives, to their dogs and their loves.

## YOUR FINAL MESSAGE

When sharing a meal, be it a slice of pizza or the bone of a steak or the end of a child's string cheese, that is communion.

When giving birth and caring for and raising and teaching a child, that is faith.

When living with a dog, such as you, in a home, sharing a space and a life and a single heart, that is a covenant.

When looking into your eyes, really looking as if expecting to find something there, they will see the face of God.

When they come home and you greet them at the door, no matter the circumstance, no matter the time or place or loss, your tail and body and tongue and spirit are in motion, and that love is Grace, that greeting Shalom.

And that, finally, is the greeting you will end on for all the people who have ever come in contact with a dog. Simply and forever: Shalom.

# ABOUT THE AUTHOR

Terry Bain (a.k.a. He Who Leaves the Seat Up So That You Might Drink) wrote this book when he should have been throwing the tennis ball. He is a freelance writer, book designer, and teacher. He won an O. Henry Award for short fiction and was named a Book Magazine Newcomer in 2003. He lives in a modest pack in Spokane, Washington, that includes his wife, two children, two dogs, and a cat.